MONEY AND MANIFESTING II

Dyan Garris

MONEY AND MANIFESTING II
BY DYAN GARRIS

www.DyanGarris.com

Journeymakers, Inc.

© 2014 Dyan Garris

All rights reserved,
including the right of reproduction in whole or in part in any form.

Published in the United States of America.

No part of this book may be used or reproduced in any manner whatsoever without the written permission of the publisher.

The characters in this book are entirely fictional and the sole creation of the author. Any resemblance to anyone living or not living is unintentional and purely coincidental.

Recipes © 2007 Dyan Garris – *Voice of the Angels Cookbook – Talk to Your Food! Intuitive Cooking*

Cover art by Limebar Creative

ISBN 13: 978-0-9841142-9-0

Printed in the United States of America

Money and Manifesting II is dedicated to all fellow travelers on the path. May your journey be easy and your life be blessed in all possible ways.

MONEY AND MANIFESTING II

PREFACE

When I first wrote Money and Manifesting in 2007 (second printing, 2010), one of my primary intentions was to present a solid framework from which people would be able to get the Law of Attraction in perspective. The Secret had become very popular at that time, and people across the planet were trying to manifest with the power of their minds, and from the place of "I want."

As we now know, there was much left out of those teachings regarding the true process of manifesting. And therefore, people became eventually frustrated, but weren't really sure exactly what was missing; only just that something definitely was. Hence, the information contained in Money and Manifesting was brought forth to help provide the missing keys.

Manifesting is a process; an integrative, 3D, multi-dimensional, mind, body, spirit process. That process is fully explored and explained in Money and Manifesting. As well, to automatically facilitate this process, the first printing of that book was on "rich," glossy paper so that when you held it in your hands, you were already bringing in the element of the emotional body. We need that emotional element to manifest, as manifesting is not linear.

For those that do not know, to that same aim, there were also seven characters introduced. Their stories intertwined. Each character represented a part of the chakra system and each also represented various patterns and belief systems that keep us stuck and keep us from effectively moving forward in life.

The fictional story was wrapped around the factual information and the chakra information. I did this purposefully so that the brain would have to make a shift from right brain to left brain; from emotion to intellect, from the bigger picture to the more linear, and vice versa. As manifesting isn't a linear process, that movement and integration between left brain—right brain also helps set a foundation for the process.

Along the way, people have written me and expressed a sincere interest in the story of the characters. Although they were examples of where we get stuck, their stories evoked connection and emotion, and that was very much a primary goal.

In the years that have passed since the first printing of Money and Manifesting, our characters have grown and changed. They have learned many lessons and have moved forward on the path just as you have.

Here we pick up the thread of their stories, and as such once again are able to see ourselves reflected. It is through that reflection, and through the emotional and spiritual threads that weave all of us together, that we have the platform for further transformation.

In Money and Manifesting II, instead of focusing on the entire chakra system, we focus mainly on the root as that is where we currently find ourselves stuck and entrenched. And that is where manifesting begins. So let's get to it.

CONTENTS

NICHOLAS – A STORM IS BREWING................. 9
CARLA...13
DEEPLY SEATED INGRAINED PATTERNS 16
THE ROOT CHAKRA/WHY IT'S SO IMPORTANT... 17
OTHER ENERGIES THAT RESIDE IN THE ROOT ...20
PATTERN: ENTITLEMENT 22
PATTERN: ENABLING 26
BOBBY 33
PATTERN: PROCRASTINATION 35
PATTERN: ANGER AND JEALOUSY.....................40
PATTERN: JUDGEMENT AND PREDJUDICE..........41
KENETHA..46
KARMA 51
LUCKY..52
ASTROLOGY...57
BARBARA..58
PATTERN: FEAR AND IMMOBILIZATION 63
GRATITUDE 67
A TALE OF WOE..68
EGO & EGO PERCEPTIONS 88
LUCKY..89
BARBARA..92
MINI SEAFOOD QUICHE 93
WHAT DOES FOOD HAVE TO DO WITH MONEY? .96
PATTERN: SELF SABOTAGE..............................98
REPEATING PATTERNS 102
PERCEPTIONS OF VALUE 108
ATTITUDES TOWARD FREE 110
SPIRITUALITY & SPIRITUAL GUIDANCE 112
BARBARA.. 114
FRANKIE... 117
WHAT'S WRONG WITH THE LOA? 119
CREATING YOUR LIFE FROM WHO YOU ARE 120
ALIGNMENT 122

BARBARA	122
FRANKIE	125
YOUR LIFE'S PURPOSE	130
PASSION	131
WHAT DO YOU MEAN CO-CREATE?	131
CONNECT THE DOTS	132
CREATING FROM YOUR ROOT	133
I DON'T KNOW WHO I AM	133
WHAT WEATLHY PEOPLE KNOW	135
THE ENERGY OF CREATION	136
MONEY: A PRIMARY RELATIONSHIP	137
NICHOLAS	139
ANTHONY	139
ELAYNE	141
DESERVING	142
LUCKY & BARBARA	143
HEALTHY BOUNDARIES	148
PATTERNS	149
DYSFUNCTIONAL PATTERNS IN FAMILIES	150
CARLOS	152
BARBIE & FRANKIE	155
CARLA	159
CARLOS	160
ELAYNE	162
ANTHONY	162
FRANKIE & BARBIE	163
ANTHONY	164
FRANKIE	164
CARLA	165
WHAT IS POWER	166
EPILOGUE	169
DATE MUFFINS	171

NICHOLAS – A STORM IS BREWING

Nicholas Fortuna stared out pensively at the swirling ocean from atop his master bedroom balcony. His mysterious cobalt blue eyes grew as dark as the sky was becoming. The churning sea reminded him of a frothy, green, bubbling caldron, not that he'd ever seen one of those. The oversized French doors behind him rattled ever so slightly as the wind began a low howl.

Unconcerned, comfortably naked, and sprawled out on his plush Euro style lounger, he took another deep swig of Tutankhamun Ale, holding it there in his mouth for a minute, almost like a fine wine, savoring its rich-bodied, slightly caramel flavor. It wasn't meant for everyone, this exclusive, faintly sweet beer. Not only was it outrageously expensive, it was, after all, a distinctly royal brew, fit for the ancient Egyptian Pharaohs. *Yes, it was definitely good to be rich.*

The past few years had been magnificent for Nicholas. His heart had softened and his luck had improved almost immediately upon taking up with his girlfriend, aptly named Lucky, and also apparently from the very fruity Bobby Dubois' famous Feng Shui cures he'd had performed a few years ago.

It had been worth putting up with the man's stealing of his silverware and gold encrusted clothes hangers, just to get his house, and therefore, his life, ostensibly, in perfect harmony with "universal flow." *Seriously, did the man think he didn't know? Everyone knew.*

Bobby considered this thievery as part of his payment or some such weirdness. At the end of every job he would always steal something from each of his clients; a little memento that he felt entitled to take.

It made no sense to Nicholas because it wasn't as if the guy wasn't paid handsomely for his talents. He was. And Bobby enjoyed almost legendary status among the rich and famous for his special brand of Feng Shui cures. Maybe no one really understood this "magic" except Bobby himself. But whatever he did, it worked. And so while the thievery was beyond infuriating, it was still worth invariably having some extraneous items go missing from your home after a Bobby Dubois visit in order to get the desired results.

Whatever, Nicholas thought. *There wasn't any such thing as integrity anymore was there?* It didn't seem to be such a valuable commodity. *After all, where did it get you? It didn't make you rich.* And thievery aside, he still didn't understand the whole gay thing and never would. *Definitely weird.*

As one consequence of the Feng Shui treatments, at least in his mind, Nicholas' last two pictures had grossed mega-millions. He was definitely and unequivocally a superstar. And he wouldn't have to worry about money ever again. Never. He felt entirely secure. He should be happy. And he had been happy. But now Lucky was gone. Maybe these Feng Shui things wore off or something. He made a mental note to have his new assistant call that Dubois person and find out.

Ultimately, he thought, frowning, *Lucky just didn't understand him*. She didn't understand his way of life. She wasn't an actress or a model, although she was pretty enough to be either. She was from the other side of the tracks so to speak. And even though he had his own humble beginnings, yes, he would admit to being a bit of a snob.

But *damn it*, he thought, he was *entitled* to be whatever he wanted to be. He had *earned* it. She just didn't understand the pressure he was under to always perform, to look his best, to be perfect, to have the perfect smile, to be charming, and to have the perfect life.

And the women. They were always there, throwing themselves at him carelessly like silk scarves. Women of all ages. Didn't seem to matter. *So he was not supposed to like this?* It was part of why he signed up for this gig

Lucky just didn't get it. Not at all. His heart was with her. And it was a very big heart. *Why wasn't that enough?*

He had come home last night from a location shoot in Italy to find her and all of her brightly colored clothes gone. The emptiness he felt in his heart echoed dully throughout the sprawling ocean-side estate which now seemed as if it were engulfed in a misty grey fog. She had told him she was leaving, that she wouldn't be there when he returned, but he hadn't allowed himself to believe that she would really do it. *After all, where would she possibly go that was better than right here with him?*

Okay, maybe he was a bit of a narcissist. But his therapist seemed to agree that there was a difference between that and a healthy ego. He wouldn't be who he was or where he was without that ego. That much he knew. *Why didn't Lucky know it?*

Nicholas sighed deeply as he stood up and finished the exquisite ale. He flexed his equally exquisite abs, mostly to make sure they were still there, and noted the dark clouds gathering rapidly now. Yes, a storm was indeed brewing. He gathered up the empty bottle and went inside.

CARLA

Carla Ortega impatiently brushed a wayward strand of thick, wildly wavy dark hair from her smooth brow. She frowned in perplexed consternation at the Tarot card she had just pulled randomly out of the deck. Her precious Tarot cards always told her the truth. And Carla didn't like the truth she saw before her at the moment.

Dios Mío, Carlita! Are you with those cards again?" Her handsome husband, Carlos, who was waiting for her to make some dinner, sounded just as annoyed as she felt. *Well, why not? What was so unusual?* They were, of course, soul mates, so connected and each feeling what the other felt. The truth was that Carla was never apart from these cards and in fact even tucked them underneath her soft, satin pillow every night. *In a strange way*, she thought, *the cards were another soul mate.*

Si, mi amor. Uno momento! I will be right there. She could almost hear his hungry, empty stomach growling all the way from the next room in their rambling beachfront estate.

Not so long ago they had navigated through some very rough financial waters when Carlos had trouble passing his bar exam and almost got fired from the American law firm that had believed so strongly in him. But they were now "sitting prettiest," Carla thought to herself, her English still, always, and perhaps forever a little offbeat.

Her Carlos was now a very important *abogado*, a lawyer for the rich and famous. They had been able to buy the oceanfront home Carla had always dreamed of. And Carla's little store, Carla's Tarot Dream was indeed another realized dream.

It had been a lifelong ambition of hers to open the quaint metaphysical shop where she did Tarot readings for customers and sold beautiful angel figurines, shining crystals, the best angel cards, and all things spiritual. She didn't care if such things were perhaps looked down upon by the more elite people her husband worked with and for. They just didn't understand, and Carla didn't care if they did or not. She had "exotic gypsy" imprinted on her very *soul,* and that she would change for no one.

Yes, the Universe had indeed been very kind to Carla and Carlos, who at one time had believed their trials and tribulations were the result of being punished for their naughty, extramarital affair. Well, obviously they must have now atoned in the eyes of the Gods, because Carla and Carlos were very lucky, living happily inside of their own dream and listening to the beautiful music of the ocean every day.

As if to cement this truth, and affirm it in some manner, she made the sign of the cross against her chest, gazed upward with her almond shaped, amber colored eyes, and whispered a grateful thanks to the powers that be for all of their good fortune.

Certainly, nothing could ever possibly happen to shatter their safety after all they had been through so far, and she would hear the music of the ocean every day of her life until it was time to go home. But for her that time was far away, Carla knew, so she wasn't worried about death at all. Yes, she would live happily here in this vision most lovely until the end of her days.

Shaking her head slightly as if to clear it, Carla slid the Tarot card, the Five of Pentacles, swiftly back into the deck. *Penalidad*. Penalty, hardship. . .punishment. It was not a good card. *No! Not ever again.* She underlined that statement in her mind. And hoping fervently that she would never see that ugly, unfortunate card again, she hastened into the kitchen to greet her handsome love.

DEEPLY SEATED INGRAINED PATTERNS

Most everyone on the planet today who uses money as a means of exchange has a distorted sense of the concept of money. We have this because as a collective consciousness, we ourselves have distorted it. We *created* the distortion in the fabric and we wonder why it's wrinkled.

Money has become way more than a means of exchange. In our current illusion it has become power. Whether it will stay that way remains to be seen. But imagine for a moment what we could create if we put our positivity on as a collective, instead of our cloak of fear and illusion, and decided to live in a totally different reality, one in which money did not equate to power, or happiness, or the magical panacea to everyone's problems. But, for whatever reasons, this is what we put our focus on creating and so that IS indeed our current reality.

Although anything is possible, and great shifts occur every day on many different levels, I am not sure we can change this perception as it is now so deeply ingrained. And maybe we don't want to. Pretty much our entire world functions this way. So if we can't change it, or more importantly, *won't* change it, we therefore need to learn to live with and make this energy work for us rather than us working for *it.*

There is a way to get what we want—more than one way in fact—working within the frameworks we've designed for ourselves and currently live within. But the way to get there begins with core patterns and belief systems that reside in our root, because the *energy of money also resides in our root.*

So let us work on our root chakras and start by examining some of the deeply ingrained patterns that live there. We already know from *Money and Manifesting* that manifesting is a whole body and multi-dimensional process. But again, since the energy of money lives in the root, let's break through some of these root chakra patterns in order to free up some of that energy so that we can take some steps forward on the path.

THE ROOT CHAKRA AND WHY IT'S SO IMPORTANT

The energy of creation resides in the root. Period. This is the single, most important statement you can take away from this book. If you remember nothing else, remember that.

Many have been previously taught that the energy of creation is in the second chakra. This simply is not true. It's not that the sacral chakra is not involved at all in the creation process. It certainly is, just as all of the other chakras are as well. But the energy of creation starts in the root and rises up through the rest of the chakras.

The second chakra functions as a "house" for the energy of creation. The second chakra is where the energy of creation *gestates.*

The root chakra is where the nourishment from the Earth rises up and feeds the plant—the rest of the body. Again, the *energy of creation resides in the root*. And that has everything to do with your money and your manifesting. Remember, the energy of *money* also resides in the root. So just as in any relationship, these two need to learn to get along and function as a team.

What I find daily in speaking with people is that there is much confusion about where the root chakra is, and what its purpose is. What we often see for a description of the root chakra is: "The root chakra is located at the base of the spine." And therefore, people tell me they are looking behind them—sometimes in their rear or butt or lower back—for this chakra, instead of where it is actually located.

The root chakra extends directly down from the genital area. It isn't behind you. It's not in front of you. Think of it as a root or grounding cord, like an electrical cord—or like the root of a plant—that comes straight down from your body, and that you plug directly into the earth.

So when we talk about "grounding," you may additionally want to think of this root as a three-pronged plug (as we have literally upgraded our electrical systems here on the planet), and ground then directly down from the root chakra, as well as from the bottoms of both your feet. The three pronged plug, after all, is a better, more powerful, upgraded version of our old two prong plugs. So let us follow suit.

Desire begins in the root. Kundalini rises from the root. And while all things weave together in many ways, and on many levels, in the process of creation, it all starts with the root. If it didn't, we would have a bunch of eggs sitting around in 2nd chakra ovaries doing nothing.

It's important to know what other energies are in there too, because if you're blocked in the root, there are many other processes that can get blocked up. And that's where we get stuck in life and feel as if we can't get off "square one." The root chakra is literally "square one."

For example, a person can have many creative ideas (energy that emanates from the sacral chakra), and can gestate them, where they spin around and around, sometimes even for years, yet not be able to "birth" them. So it's important to keep the root chakra as clear as possible as it's analogous to a birth canal.

Now let's delve deeper. What other energies live in the root?

OTHER ENERGIES THAT RESIDE IN THE ROOT

The chakra system is a complex network, but it's not difficult to understand. The chakras are not unto themselves. They are all made to work together, just as everything in our bodies is designed so. And we in our interactions with each other are designed to do so as well. Our relationship with our chakras can be as simple or as complex as we choose.

The chakras are energy centers in our etheric bodies, connected by a pipeline—the spine. And the energy of one chakra connects to the energy of the one above and so on. So some of the energies spill over, but each chakra has a definite purpose and houses specific energies.

For a complete explanation and thorough discussion of each chakra and what its purpose is, please read *Money and Manifesting*. For our purposes here, we are mainly addressing the energies that dwell in the 1st or root chakra, because that is where the energy of money lives. And that is where many people are completely blocked and stuck with their money issues *and* with their manifesting. Here is a list of some of the other main energies, besides money, that lie in the root:

* Fear, superstitions, & belief in karma
* Entitlement
* Co-dependence & enabling
* Ego & narcissism
* Procrastination
* Desire
* Sex
* Shame
* Addictions
* Control issues
* Survival
* Abuse and self-abuse
* Primal fear and safety
* Victimhood
* Tribal/family patterns & group acceptance
* Sense of "groundedness" & ability to ground
* Sense of purpose/self-worth
* Anger & jealousy
* Judgment
* Kundalini energy
* Divine right to create and co-create

Essentially, anything that pertains to the "root of the matter" lives in this chakra.

PATTERN: ENTITLEMENT

What is entitlement and how do we identify it? Entitlement is a quite deeply seated belief system. It is one of the strongly held belief systems that stands in our way of creating our lives the way we desire them to be, i.e., effective manifesting. And it is one of the embedded belief systems that stands in our way of creating money.

At its base, simplistic form, entitlement says that the world owes you something, or someone or something owes you something. Partly it's based on the misguided notion that whatever you think you've put out there is going to come back to you (that *is* what we have been taught to believe about karma), *and* come back to you in this lifetime, *and* in a certain way—often in a way in which you dictate. But the truth is that while you can definitely try, you cannot ultimately tell the Universe what to do.

Entitlement often says you've been wronged in some manner and so you are entitled to receive a, b, c. It says, "I've paid my dues, or paid for whatever, and now because of that, I am owed such and such in return."

It's easy for us to get stuck there because we are taught from very early on "we get what we pay for." We are taught "what goes around comes around," and "an eye for an eye."

It's a pretty screwed up value system actually, because that is not necessarily true. And this belief system does not necessarily create the equitable foundation of "fair exchange of energy" that is a necessary ingredient in all of effective manifesting. But that viewpoint of how energy *supposedly* works is also deeply ingrained through many layers in our collective consciousness.

We do have an entire legal/justice system based upon these "owed" and "owing" concepts. I'm not saying it's wrong. I'm saying that if you find yourself stuck in life, creating the same miserable situation over and over again, then look to the underlying belief systems that led you there. From there it is your choice whether or not you want to keep creating more of the same or change the vibration and the pattern at the root level and attract something totally different.

As well, entitlement is very often confused with "opening to receive," or just plain "receiving." Entitlement says "I am *entitled* to receive." And that's where the trouble starts.

Those steeped in entitlement may have no idea that they are stewing in that brew, partly because they are entitled, and partly because, well, it just very simply works for them. Or, because it works for them, they will ignore the truth of it and just stay there.

Entitlement creates a framework in which the "receiver" over and over again creates a scenario of victimhood, all the while believing they are *not* a victim, yet fully expecting to be saved and/or compensated for the imbalance or "wrongs." And there are usually plenty of people who are willing to engage in the "saving."

And, so on and on the pattern of entitlement goes, until one day—particularly true for anyone on the path of the "light worker"—the entitlement door gets more and more narrow and the energy no longer is resonant with the required transformation. And there we get stuck, somewhere between the partially open door and the opening. We become unable to move, paralyzed by the pattern.

Whether we want to hear this or not, the bottom line is that entitlement is a person having a tantrum which often sounds like this:

"I've helped so many people. . ."

Or:

"I've given a lot of whatever, and so I am entitled to sit here and receive from others no matter who it is or what it costs them."

Or:

"It's my turn."

Or:

"The Universe takes care of me because . . ."

And it's the "because" that is the operative word in this equation. The truth is that the Universe takes care of *all*. It does not take care of you *because* you have done or performed x, y, or z.

Truly, unless we are a helpless infant, we are *entitled* to nothing, and we are completely responsible for our choices and what we choose to create in our lifetimes as a consequence of those choices. So, to begin to move yourself out of the entitlement trap, go back and examine and reflect upon all of your choices. Then take full responsibility for them. No excuses.

On a spiritual level, both individually and as a collective, we are being asked now to grow up whether we want to or not. We are being asked to examine our patterns at the base, at the root, and *do* something about them. What worked in childhood does not work in maturity. We are being asked to rise above and to shed the garb of childhood. It no longer fits.

We are being asked to transform the lower into the higher on *all* levels. And the truth is that we can transform absolutely nothing, not even the lint that may be there, from the space of crawling around on the floor of entitlement. We must stand and walk.

Entitlement says a lot of things. *What do you say?*

PATTERN: ENABLING

To enable or not to enable? That is the question. Are you an enabler?

Years ago when I was a young teen, thirteen to be exact, there was a girl named Alice in one of my classes. In this particular class we had an assignment to sew an article of clothing. Alice was brand new to our school and didn't have any friends yet. She was quite different from the rest of us with her teased, dirty, dishwater blonde hair piled up high to the sky and her shiny, jet black high heeled boots. I had never seen anyone like her. But in my own way I didn't exactly "blend" either. So I felt some sort of odd vibrational simpatico with Miss Alice.

Alice informed the teacher she did not have any money to buy the necessary material to make the item. "I don't have no money," she stated empathically. I didn't know how to then, perhaps, but now I could accurately describe the look in Alice's narrow green eyes as defensive and defiant rather than ashamed or downtrodden. *At least she had spirit.*

Alice was a tall girl for her age, the teacher not so much, and with the glossy boots Alice was—even with her slouchy posture—therefore, at eye level with the instructor for this exchange. The teacher stared directly back at the girl with not one iota of compassion in her own eyes, and told Alice she understood, but to pass the class, she would have to come up with it somehow. It was, after all, only $5.00.

I remember observing this interchange with great curiosity. *Sometimes $5.00 is a lot of money.* My heart went out to this girl, Alice. But there was something about the *way* she made the statement that stuck with me. And still does. It was almost. . . triumphant. There seemed to be some kind of strange, inexplicable power in "I don't have no money." Or at least Alice perceived that to be true.

At a young age, I had the fortunate experience of being able to work in one of my father's establishments. So I did not receive an allowance. I had a job. I earned my own money, understood money, knew how the energy of money functioned. And from that very young age, I was able to buy myself (and expected to, actually), personal necessities and other things without relying on others to provide them. That early independence was such a gift on so many levels, and one that would stand me in good stead in later years. Because of that gift I had a firm grip on who I was, and a firm belief in my innate ability to create, no matter what the circumstance.

When I went home from school that day, I sought out my mother. I told her about Alice having no money to do her assignment. I told her I was going to give Alice the money to make the clothing article. I wasn't asking my mother's permission to do so, because after all, my money earned by my own hard work was mine to do with as I chose and I didn't need her permission. I was seeking her opinion.

My mother looked at me in astonishment. She told me that was very kind of me and asked why I would want to do such a thing. Even back then it didn't strike me as odd or unnatural to be kind to another or to help someone who had fallen upon hard times. So I surmised there must be something else going on here. And I was right.

I told my mother I just wanted to help this Alice out. I realized that everyone was not as fortunate as we were. I felt sorry for her that she wasn't able to make this item due to her circumstances. I felt that if I gave her this money, gave her this *opportunity,* she would be able to shine even brighter than her boots, pass the class, *create* something useful from her own hand, do well. *Didn't everyone want to do well?*

My mother told me that *no, everyone didn't want to do well,* and said that it sounded to her as if Alice was simply trying to get out of completing the assignment. "She's using it as an excuse to not do the work," my mother said.

It was my turn to be astonished, because truly this hadn't occurred to me; the idea completely foreign. I have four planets in Virgo. *Doesn't everyone like to work?*

I asked my mother if she thought it would make a difference if I loaned the girl the money rather than give it to her. *Was that the problem?* My mother smiled a wry little smile, raised her eyebrows slightly, and told me that it probably wouldn't make any difference. But she encouraged me to do whatever I felt was the right thing to do.

The next day at school, in that class, I told both Alice and the teacher that I was going to provide the money so Alice could make the clothing. I was so happy with this announcement, which came directly from my heart. From my mind I was thinking that Alice would also be so relieved and happy to have the pressure off, and she would be able to complete the assignment, feel her own sense of independence, and *do well.*

I was in for a rude awakening, however. Alice took the money I handed her. She did indeed snatch it from my hand. And it was the teacher's turn to look triumphant. But Alice gave me daggers in return—green eyes flashing hatefully—and in her brief remaining time at our school, she never spoke to me or acknowledged me again, even though our lockers were next to each other.

Apparently I had unknowingly spoiled her plan of using "lack" as an excuse to do nothing. But that wasn't my intention. My intention was to provide a *tool* and a means for her to get out of the place that she said she was in. And that place didn't seem like a very good place to me. *What did I know?* The truth was that it worked for her.

That day I also learned a valuable lesson in the difference between enabling and assisting. *You can lead a horse to water, show him the water, or even provide the water in a fancy bucket. But ultimately you cannot make him drink even if you know he is thirsty. . .and even if he knows he is thirsty.*

Sometimes people only need a leg up in order to gain a little traction to get over the bump in the road. And other times people just want to do what they want to do and in the way they want to do it. . .or not do it as the case may be. And that may not coincide with your own plan or vision of the way things ought to shape up. Everyone has their own agenda, lessons to learn, and sacred contracts to fulfill.

We truly cannot help anyone who refuses to be helped, who doesn't want to get out of the place they are in because it works for them, or who has made a lifelong career out of using "victimhood" and "lack" to get on in life. There are many who are quite good at and excel at such a career. And so much so that through the hazy smokescreen we may not at first see the underlying pattern, as I didn't see it with Alice all those years ago.

But we can ultimately discern the truth by examining the facts and the fruits. Examine the way in which whatever it is we have provided or put forth is treated, used, not used, respected, disrespected, honored or dishonored.

In this career, there are indeed "professional victims" who at the same time are "bosses," of their perceived powerlessness, as again, this energy pattern *works for them*. When you're the "boss of powerlessness," you are at least in control of something, and you learn to use that energy to manipulate instead of to create. This pattern is what keeps people stuck. *It's not forward moving.* We are designed to function at our highest and best, to create and co-create, not to manipulate.

The decision to change this way of being and relating must come from within, not from the outside. *You can't make it for them.* They will only change it when the pattern quits working for them, stops producing for them; *when utter misery replaces entitlement.* From your side, it is a choice as to whether you will enable or assist or neither. It's a choice.

Helping, being part of a team, or engaging in a healthy relationship, is not the same as enabling someone to continue on in their pattern. *You cannot fix anyone.* And enabling keeps YOU stuck in a non-forward moving pattern of co-dependence.

While Alice never spoke to me again, I have met her many times on the path. I smile, wave, say, "Hi. You haven't changed much in all these years." And I keep on going. *What do you do?*

BOBBY

Bobby's assistant texted him. Bobby was rich now, and that entitled him to certain perks. One of those perks was a *person*. Everyone needed a *person* to do all of the things that one didn't want to do and so one could concentrate on their work. *And* on making money, of course.

Bobby loved making money. And making money was what he was doing these days. *Lots and lots of money.* He'd long ago gotten rid of that idiotic boyfriend of his, the one who'd squandered Bobby's inheritance through his equally idiotic gambling problem. And he'd just recently gotten rid of Brian, his boyfriend for the past few years, and former *person* to one Mr. Nicholas Fortuna.

Or maybe Brian had gotten rid of him. *What did it matter anyway?* Brian was gone. Money was Bobby's main focus, and why shouldn't it be? Everyone was focused on it, it seemed.

Like a broken record, these spiritual gurus were always telling everyone to clear, clear, clear out the past and bring in the new, new, new. Well, that's what he'd done. Goodbye and good riddance to the past. And hello to more and more money. That's all he cared about. Money was power. And if Brian didn't understand that, well, so what? He, Bobby Dubois, was *not* going to be in the "have not" category. Not ever again. He even had hired an accountant to ensure that his success stayed intact.

Bobby glanced at the text. *Great.* That chiseled hunk of a man, Nicholas Fortuna wanted to talk to him. Even though it felt like a formal summons on some level, a brief wave of momentary excitement coursed through his body. Not that Nicholas had any kind of interest in him whatsoever. *Goodness, the man was a flaming homophobe.*

But he was still nice to look at, what with those deep, dark, navy blue eyes; immense pools of lusciousness you could get completely lost in. Not to mention those broad shoulders, and infamous, rock hard abs. No one should have a body like that. It was insane. *Should be illegal.*

Bobby sighed a deep sigh. *A man could dream couldn't he?* And when it came to Nicholas, well, yes, he had certainly done that plenty of times. But still, the man was irritating, particularly now, when he was trying to forget about all things "Brian." He'd call Nicholas later.

PATTERN: PROCRASTINATION

Why do we procrastinate? And is procrastination a problem? What is it?

Procrastination is a habit. And it's one of many deeply ingrained patterns of behavior that keeps us from moving forward. So, yes, it's definitely a problem if you want to move forward on your path. Let's examine the role of procrastination in manifesting.

Procrastination, by its very nature, ultimately creates stress. Stress blocks our ability to effectively manifest, create, and co-create. We can't see past the wall we have created.

Habitual procrastination can actually be destructive rather than just inert. Think about what you're really creating in the present moment when you procrastinate. Since everything is connected, by procrastinating, one of the things you're doing inside of the non-doing, is setting off a chain reaction of a slew of missed opportunities. Even though everything weaves together for the highest good, you have still created a void of sorts, limitation of sorts, in terms of opportunities.

Procrastination is a form of "negative manifesting." Some people do this completely unconsciously and are then left to wonder why things aren't working out the way they envision. When you procrastinate you are working against the flow.

Many people want gratification in the present, not in the future. Unfortunately, this is a child's perspective, and the universe is requiring us to grow out of that. If our present is grossly uncomfortable, we may have a tendency to procrastinate; to project our dreams and visions into a future where we perceive things will be less uncomfortable and maybe even quite comfortable, as in, "When my ship comes in. . ."

But the truth is that we create *everything* that happens next from where we are right now in this moment. This is one reason why it's so important to come into the "now." The power in the "now" is not just a bunch of New Age mumbo-jumbo. It is a necessary ingredient in the process of manifesting.

Some people adopt procrastination as a lifestyle choice. These are the ones who don't pay their bills on time, don't file their taxes on time, don't ever show up on time. Let's examine why this occurs.

Simply stated, at the bottom of the procrastination barrel, and therefore at the root, is also some kind of fear. This could be any kind of fear. One could be afraid of failure, afraid of success, afraid of not being perfect, or afraid of the loss of control. And it doesn't matter, because vibrationally speaking, fear is fear. *The universe does not differentiate between different kinds of fear*. The vibration of fear resides in the root chakra, which we know now, also contains the energy of money. Fear blocks your ability to manifest, to create, to move forward, to make money.

As well, on an emotional level, we procrastinate because of the way we *feel* about doing a particular task. But often we end up feeling worse about not doing it. Procrastination rests on the laurels of avoiding unpleasant tasks, but the truth is it creates more unpleasantness just by its very nature.

To get things in perspective, and help to propel yourself forward, try first to examine with your mind, the *emotions* associated with whatever it is you don't want to do or don't want to face. Are you afraid of something? Does not doing whatever it is in a timely fashion make you feel empowered in some way or in control?

Then with your mind, disassociate from the emotions surrounding whatever it is. And then just *do* it. Your emotional body will thank you for it later and so most probably will your wallet.

* * * * *

Successful people have some things in common. One of those things is that whatever it is, they tend to just "get 'er done." They are driven to achieve. But do successful people have more time than anyone else has? No. They just engage in time management. The underlying belief system (good, bad, indifferent, right or wrong), is that "time is money."

There are many reasons we have chosen to divide up our Earth time into small pieces of hours, minutes, and seconds. One of those reasons is so we can choose to engage in effective time management. With this model, in order to not become overwhelmed, we are able to break our lives and our tasks up into smaller, more manageable pieces.

Obviously we can't be all things to all people and we can't do all things at one time. So effective time management becomes an important tool, just like any other tool that has been provided to us. But using "poor" time management as an excuse to procrastinate can block your way forward and keep you from becoming "rich."

Another reason people procrastinate is due to some bizarre misconception of being in control or needing to be in control. This is twisted, because if you wait until you have no more time to complete the task, you have just created limitation. *Do you understand?* We cannot create anything forward moving from a place of limitation. But you, yourself, have created this limitation by your procrastination. You are in your own way. *Do you see?*

Procrastination holds hands with excuses and meanders down the path to nowhere. An excuse is denial of some truth, a pushing off of something you know you should do now, but for whatever reason don't do, and/or a shifting of personal responsibility onto someone or something else. Excuses are self-delusions that keep us locked in the cell—and that is not just the proverbial "jail cell," it's also at the cellular level. Procrastination becomes our "cell mate," and keep us locked away from realizing our full potential.

The bottom line is that procrastination on any level is dishonoring and disrespectful to ourselves, to our incarnation and to what we came to do, to others, and to the Creator. Procrastination impedes our ability to create, and therefore our ability to co-create. It affects our relationships, our jobs and careers, and our whole lives in general.

Why, unless we are so completely steeped in entitlement that we cannot see it this way, would anyone be so nonchalant about the gift of life that we would truly believe we have all the time in the world?

PATTERN: ANGER AND JEALOUSY

Jealousy is a base emotion, not necessarily because it vibrates so low on the vibrational scale, which it does, but because it also resides in the root. We may believe it resides in the heart chakra, hence the old saying, "green with envy." (The color of the heart chakra - and the color of money in the U.S.A. - is green).

But the truth is jealousy emanates up from the root and rises up through the chakras to eventually get stuck in the heart. In order to effectively manifest, we do also need to at some point engage the passion of the heart. But how can we do that effectively and whole-"heartedly" if we have created blockages there through jealousy? Jealousy serves no purpose.

Jealousy can also get stuck in another chakra as well, and that is the "head" chakra, or 6th chakra. But remember, jealousy first emanates from the root. As such, many times at first, we can't—or don't—identify what we're feeling as "jealousy." But sometimes we can find ourselves having inexplicable resistance to doing something for a particular person or with a particular person. Look carefully then and determine whether or not you may be vibrating to jealousy. It can sneak up on us and it definitely can hide down there in the root and disguise itself under a murky shroud of denial.

But as all of the energy in the lower chakras does rise up to the upper chakras, sometimes then we can see jealousy in someone's eyes. This is why we have the expression "green eyed monster," to describe the emotion of jealousy.

Anger is a base emotion as well, and one of the things we're doing here on the planet is engaging in the attempt to master our emotions and our base physical nature. The goal is to balance mind, body, and spirit and create a harmonious experience.

When we're angry, we could say we're "seeing red." (The color of the root chakra is red). And in this anger, we become blinded to a lot of truths that keep us from manifesting, and consequently can also keep us from making money.

PATTERN: JUDGEMENT AND PREDJUDICE

Sometimes we may think we are the most open-minded person there is. But if we examined this belief about ourselves at the core, we may discover something else entirely.

Our value systems form very quickly when we are children. These we adopt from our caretakers, parents, or those around us. We also adopt them as well from our experiences.

Nobody comes in here remembering much of anything. We don't know who we are. We can't even speak and we communicate at first with our emotions. So while we do come in with sacred contracts and an agenda to fulfill those, most of what we learn at first and, therefore, at the root, is taught to us.

In order to get to the bottom of any blockage, we first have to get to the root. And that can be challenging, not because we don't necessarily want to get to the root, but because we may be blinded to certain truths by our judgments, prejudices, and intolerance.

Judgments are not the same as opinions. A judgment is when we look at something and deem it to be a certain way based upon what we think we see or what we think we know.

For example—and this is a very basic example—we may see a pretty blonde girl and decide that she must be dumb. This is a *judgment.* Upon speaking to this girl, and getting to know her a little bit, we may form the *opinion* that she is quite intelligent.

Another example is that we may see a group of young men congregating together and decide they are in a gang. But our *opinion* of them may change when we find out they are in a church choir and just waiting for their ride home. Or our opinion of them may change if they offer to change our flat tire or help us in some unexpected way. In this instance we open up to being able to see their hearts rather than the outer shell exterior or what we believe we see.

Further then, we may see a person with a swarthy complexion and decide—however irrationally—that person must be a terrorist. Our *opinion* may change when we find out they just came back from Florida and they have a very good tan.

We may encounter a homeless person and judge them to be a no-good bum. But later if we find out that this person was a doctor who lost his home, health, and practice in the housing bubble debacle, our opinion, and perhaps our resulting actions or reaction, could surely change.

It's important to understand that our judgments and prejudices are based upon some kind of fear, some kind of deep seated belief system or pattern that tells us if this is so, then this other thing must be so.

Our judgments are not necessarily what is true. And even though we are entitled to them, our opinions are not necessarily what is true. In any situation, to get to the truth of the matter, one must first get to the *root.*

We are masters at fooling ourselves, particularly when it comes to things we don't want to face in ourselves or change. And those things are usually things that require change at a base level, i.e., a change in pattern, addiction, habit, perception, or perspective. We can make up our minds to change something, but if we don't change things at the root, whatever it is won't change at all because it can't.

Change is never easy because we love our comfort zones. We're comfortable there. We feel justified in dwelling there. Who would want to be uncomfortable? We have the perception in general that change is uncomfortable and challenging.

We are creatures of habit and we love our patterns. They give us the illusion of being safe. But the truth is that we are always safe and change can be very positive and exciting. We just may not see things that way.

Life is definitely easier with money than it is without. It's relatively easy to be happy when we have money. For this reason some people marry for money. To not have to struggle for basic survival frees up a whole lot of energy in the root, and there is then space to do and create other things.

But happiness comes from within your soul. And you can *choose* to feel happiness with or without money. Marrying for money can make you miserable because you may at some point come to the realization that you're ultimately trying to have an emotional connection with a piece of paper, or many pieces of paper as the case may be.

Then again, this arrangement does work for some, particularly those who are closed off from their true emotions and view money as security or happiness.

Whatever you think you know about money, whatever you know about pieces of paper that you've collected or not collected throughout your lifetime, throw it out for right now. Put it aside long enough to think about who taught you what you know about money?

What were, or what are, *their* patterns regarding money, regarding happiness, regarding spirituality? When you get to the bottom of that, you will have many keys that can help you unlock the doors to moving forward in your life.

But examining these deep-seated belief systems requires brutal honesty, and a willingness to see and understand what you have either avoided previously, or what you haven't been able to see or understand before now. Are you willing to let go of your judgments so that you can begin to unblock yourself at the root and move forward?

KENETHA

Kenetha Barrington reported for duty at Carla's Tarot Dream promptly at 9:00 AM. Her birthday was September 11th, 1971, and she was born at precisely 12:00 PM in Darien, Connecticut, USA. Her superior skills as a professional astrologer had landed her the job of "visiting astrologer" at the popular metaphysical shop two days per week to start.

Yes, she had her own clients, but moving from the East Coast to the West Coast recently had put a huge strain on her finances. And she now needed to supplement her income.

The store seemed to be quite busy, so even though she had to split the money she earned with Carla, the owner, Kenetha expected it all to go quite well.

Kenetha wasn't surprised she was hired straight away. She was after all a Certified Astrologer, a C.A., a Level IV NCGR-PAA, and a member of the APA. She also had earned certification from the IAA, and she had several other initials, representing different modalities, to include after her name to substantiate her multiple, advanced qualifications and therefore her self-worth.

The initials were probably meaningless to anyone not familiar with the astrology world, but to her they were everything. Those initials and pieces of paper that accompanied her right to use them, proved to the world that she had paid her dues, had accomplished something in life, and most importantly, knew what she was doing. She could always earn a living with these impeccable credentials. And that she needed to do right now.

Carla Ortega, the owner of the store, seemed nice enough even if her English wasn't quite up to par. Kenetha hoped she could stand it. *What was it with these people anyway?* They came the United States and didn't bother to learn to speak the language well, or as this Carla might say, "Don't be concern well to learn the language," or some other such illiterate gibberish. *Good grief!*

In any event, here Kenetha was now. And even if she did have to grin and bear the poor English, that she would do. Certainly she had endured far worse.

* * * * *

Carla saw Kenetha from across the room. She cried out excitedly, "Welcome Kenneth!" And then Carla rushed up to her new hire exuberantly, giving her a huge, warm hug.

Kenetha was definitely not a hugger, and Carla may as well have been an overly friendly St. Bernard. Kenetha didn't want to embrace anyone else's germs on any level, and besides that, the act of hugging felt like an unwelcome invasion of her private space. It was just far too intimate for her taste. *And she was definitely not a "Kenneth."*

The awkward moment thankfully over, Kenetha, ever so mindful of her proper manners, smiled, articulated the appropriate pleasantries, and handed Carla a DVD that she had brought with her as a gift. It was a copy of *Amores Perros* (*Love is a Bitch*), an enduringly popular, award winning Mexican film.

Kenetha wasn't quite certain of Carla's actual nationality, but to her all of these Spanish speaking people were the same, so what difference did it make? In Kenetha's mind, it was like the Negros, or the African Americans, or whatever they called themselves these days. And the Orientals, or Asians, as they called themselves now. To her, they all looked alike.

Of course she didn't really care what anyone *was,* as she considered herself to be open-minded. But one thing was sure. For not the first time, she was glad she was white.

The DVD was actually a re-gift, not that Ms. Ortega would ever know that, and not that anyone would know that. Kenetha would have been horrified if anyone would have been able to guess such a thing.

She had taken the time to remove any fingerprints, polish it up, and have it re-shrink wrapped so it appeared brand new. And Kenetha had only watched it once a long time ago. So to her way of thinking, it was like new. What was the difference? In the end it was the thought that counted anyway and why waste anything?

She couldn't say she understood the movie either. As she recalled there was something about a horrible car accident that affected the lives of several people of dubious integrity. But to her the movie just seemed deep, dark, and depressing. It didn't say much for the way humanity treated one another.

What was wrong with people? Had they no decency? And there were way too many dogs in that movie too. Kenetha didn't know if Carla was a "dog person" or not, but maybe she would enjoy the movie anyway.

Kenetha couldn't say that she herself appreciated the movie's finer points, if it had any. She had only watched it because it had been Academy Award nominated and because it had been a gift from her husband, Morton.

She had married Morton for his money, this was a fact, although she didn't like to admit that even to herself. She had, after all, even signed a pre-nuptial agreement, so it certainly didn't appear that way. She had on occasion even fooled herself into believing that she loved him. But she did now definitely regret ever signing that pre-nup.

The marriage had been fine and she had been able to do, and go, and get whatever she wanted. And she only had to service Morton once a month or even less. Life had been pleasant and easy.

Somewhere along the line, however, Morton had become a bit daft. And his daftness had gotten worse as time went on. One day he cut down every single tree in their yard. She had the gardener replant all manner of greenery and shrubbery, but Morton cut it all down again.

Then he started cutting down the neighbor's trees. And he subsequently poured weed killer on any new outgrowth or any new planted foliage. He even went so far as to sneak out in the middle night to engage in this mad, nonsensical behavior. So needless to say, life was suddenly no longer pleasant and easy. And she *deserved* pleasant and easy.

When Kenetha had had enough, she left Morton in the care of his two spinster sisters, Lorraine and Deborah, and made her way forward on the path.

Kenetha felt she was entitled to happiness. She longed for greener pastures where no crazy old coot would be chopping down her trees any longer. She was totally at peace with this decision. *And why not?* It wasn't as if she owed Morton anything anyway.

KARMA

Karma, in general, is the belief that what goes around comes around. But there is a much bigger picture than that. The multi-dimensional reflection of "as above so below" is true. But often we don't get the true import of that, nor do we care about it.

What if everything you did, had effect on everything *everywhere?* Think about that for a minute. Does the microcosm affect the macrocosm? It certainly does. But we don't think about it. Why? It's perhaps easier to believe that we are autonomous.

The truth is that groups of people incarnate together for the purpose of engaging in certain lessons. "Owing," in terms of Karma, is an illusion of sorts. Those lessons we agree to, and their outcomes that we affect by our free will choices, affect our soul groups in the other realms. Our choices affect the actions of our soul groups. . . what they choose to do or not do after they depart this Earth plane.

So knowing these things, having this perspective, it is time to ratchet up a notch our notion of Karma and the purpose of our incarnations. This all requires us to get to the root because we ARE the root.

LUCKY

Lucky contemplated the astrology reading she had recently had at Carla's Tarot Dream. The shop was a pleasant, eclectic little place with good vibes, and she adored the shop owner, Carla, who she knew had once briefly worked for Nicholas. *That woman, she just knew things.* And since Lucky was in transition—or *something*—with her relationship, with everything it seemed, she felt she could use a little spiritual guidance.

She chose the astrology reading over a Tarot card reading because astrology just seemed more logical to her. It was based upon something tangible and maybe even scientific. Plus there was a special price on it just for that day. And Lucky was a very practical, frugal woman.

With slender fingers, she held one of the charts the visiting astrologer, Kenetha, had drawn up for her and gazed at it quizzically, head cocked to one side, long blond hair spilling over onto the page. Brushing the wayward, golden tress aside somewhat impatiently, she examined the strange symbols and glyphs over and over again, trying to make some sense of it all. *Really, was life this complicated?*

Lucky had come a long way from the angry woman she once was. She vividly remembered standing alone in the street gazing in horror at the rubble of her little house that her then boyfriend had burned down completely to the ground by falling asleep with his lit cig. *Lazy sloth.* Who wouldn't be angry? But as luck would have it, her luck had changed shortly thereafter, the day she dragged one Nicholas Fortuna out of a car accident moments before his car blew up to smithereens.

Since that fateful day, and over the past few years, she had worked very hard and had made somewhat of a name for herself as a successful published author. Her first novel had done quite well, she'd received a modest advance for the second, and she had even written a few screenplays. She had a new one in the works now. Nothing that Nicholas helped her with, though, and nothing had gotten in front of any big names. *Yet*.

It would happen when the time was right. She firmly believed this and knew it deep within her soul. If there was such a thing as destiny, she knew it was destined to be so. And she didn't need Nicholas' help in that department. She was good enough and talented enough and she would get this part of her life in order too.

She didn't want to owe anyone anything ever again. Not even him. *Especially not him*. That man was utterly infuriating, incredibly narcissistic, and emotionally unavailable. He didn't seem to appreciate anything she did for him.

She had straightened up her own life, her aching back, her finances, all by herself, and she was fine, thank you very much. She had been able to quit her waitress job at the diner long ago, and she had even managed to buy herself another house. It wasn't, of course, anywhere near the caliber of Nicholas' stunningly beautiful oceanfront property, but it was all hers and she cherished every square inch of it.

Small it was, but it was in a wonderful location. Included, at the back of the main house, was a cozy lock-off casita. The unit had its own private entrance and she periodically rented it out. She had completely renovated it herself, and it regularly brought good extra income, essentially paying for almost the entire monthly mortgage on the main house.

While she had been living with Nicholas, she'd rented out both the main house and the casita. But now both of those leases were over and she was coming home to an empty nest, which suited her just fine. *New beginnings.*

The house cleaners had done a brilliantly thorough job, so there was nothing for her to do in that department. And she'd go for groceries later after she visited the gym for her daily workout. Nicholas rarely cooked. He had a staff to do that for him. It had been a long time since she'd gone to the supermarket. She was looking forward to it, actually. Something normal and grounded.

Nicholas. . .what did this darn chart say about him, if anything? She tried to remember what that woman astrologer had told her about this. *Oh yes, something about true love.* How could she have forgotten that? *Hmmm.* Well, somehow she had never expected her so-called true love to be such a self-involved narcissist. That's not what every young girl imagines when she dreamily fantasizes about her true love.

Lucky didn't even know if she believed in true

love. And according to Kenetha, the astrologer, her chart was currently all squared and circled or whatever they called it. And the planet Saturn was apparently squaring or opposing Pluto or something on that order. *Too many circles and arrows and intersecting lines.* It seemed like a big mess to her and Lucky didn't like messes. Not at all.

"The chart *says*," the woman had intoned. *Yeah*, that explained it all, most specifically her recent run of what could only be called "bad luck." *The chart says.* That must be it.

Lucky had long ago stopped being a victim to anything. She wasn't about to be victimized by a piece of paper. She knew she couldn't make the chart *say* something else. But wasn't it just like a blueprint of sorts? Like Nicole Curtis, on that *Rehab Addict* program, couldn't she just move a wall or two, sand, repaint and refinish, and make things all pretty again?

ASTROLOGY

Right now the planets are dancing in the cosmos to a completely different tune than ever before. Just as the moon affects our tides, which we now know is true, the planets and their movements affect our lives. So it's helpful to know what's going on in the sky. But learning and understanding a bit about astrology, in general, can help you figure out what's going on in your own personal life as well, and more importantly, what to do about it.

I bring it up here, because personal astrology readings are first based upon your birth chart, i.e., where the planets were when you were born. So your astrology chart is both the root of who you are, and quite literally, the "higher self" of who you are at the same time. That's important to note. There is a lot that can be revealed to you in an astrology chart about who you are *and* what you came to do, and what course of action you can take regarding any of it.

One key to this big reveal, at the root level, which is where we are focused now, is to not get so narcissistically involved in this self-discovery process that you allow yourself to become victimized or paralyzed by the information. Don't form a judgment about your chart. Form an opinion. Then go from there.

So what do you do if you find out that things are not so rosy for you right now astrologically speaking? Are we really stuck with "the chart says?" Not at all.

Astrology is just a tool to help you to get to know yourself better and perhaps come to an understanding regarding others that are important to you. It can give you some new perspectives and help you get unblocked at a root level as well, if you choose to use it as a tool to that aim.

But the most important thing anyone can do about anything is to not allow yourself to get sucked into "victimhood," and especially not due to "the chart says." There is an answer to everything, a solution to everything, and often more than one. Sometimes that answer is right before you knocking on your door and sometimes you just need to dig.

BARBARA

Chomp, chomp, chomp. Knock, knock, knock. Barbara chewed noisily on her cinnamon flavored nicotine gum and pounded on Lucky's front door loudly. *Where was the woman anyway? She didn't have all day. Okay, well, maybe she did.* But the lack of immediate answer was still annoying.

Barbara—Barbie or Babs for short—was a petite woman, like her twin sister, Lucky. She looked very much like a Barbie doll with her big, china blue eyes and bright blonde hair. Unlike Lucky, she had had a boob job, Botox, and a butt lift that she didn't really need, but she'd had it anyway as it was going around at the time, so to speak.

She'd also had a slew of bad luck lately. *What was it with that anyway?* She'd have to have someone check her astrology chart. Maybe everything was all squared or conjunct or twisted up or whatever they call it.

Barbie wasn't an astrologer herself—way too much involved to get *that* certification—but up until a few years ago she'd been working as a psychic and Tarot card reader in a metaphysical bookstore. The store had gone under in the Great Recession, which was really another Great Depression, but no one dared call it that. And so she had then supplemented her income doing psychic fairs. But all had changed when she moved from Seattle, Washington to Lewistown, Montana with her then new boyfriend Brett.

She wasn't sure she was really psychic, per se, even if sometimes it did seem to her as if spirits were indeed speaking through her. She'd had a near death experience several years ago, and since that time she felt like she had seen the "light." So she labeled herself "psychic." There were many times when she even surprised herself by what she "got."

The events that led her to this predicament she now found herself in were still so traumatic that she had trouble even now facing all that had transpired. Previous to Brett, her boyfriend of the moment had fallen asleep with a lit cigarette and burned their trailer down to the ground. She had been extremely lucky to get out and had spent months recovering. Unfortunately, the boyfriend hadn't been that lucky, and neither had her big sheepdog, Fluff. It was why she now had a tiny, fluffy dog. She could simply stuff it in her bag and quickly get out of any situation, however horrendous.

Definitely Barbara had good intuition. *But what did it matter anyway if she was really psychic or not? People just wanted to hear what they wanted to hear.* And so that's what she told them, placating many a client with generalities, projections of what they'd just said or asked, and soothing words of comfort.

"You're going to be alright," and "Yes, of course he's going to call you soon. Don't you worry about that one bit," were staples in her magic bag of "psychic-ness." And all in all she was right probably about half the time, she surmised. *But so what?* She comforted people and made them feel better in the moment. And they paid her very nicely. *That's all that mattered.*

There just wasn't any psychic work up there in God's country. The other women she'd met were mostly fat cows in her estimation, like the animals they tended. And in her judgment they looked almost more masculine than the men they were married to if that were possible. She didn't have much, if anything, in common with them.

She was the queen of bling and she wasn't going to tend to any crops or livestock. *No on that*. She was definitely afraid of those cows, horses, and big horned elks. Plus they all smelled really bad. It was the kind of thing you could never quite get off you no matter how many showers you took.

She had often grown bored and lonely waiting for Brett to come home from his construction job. So she had taken up with a married rancher here and there. *None of it had meant anything, so what was the harm?* Just a meaningless fling every now and again. *So what?* Men did it all the time.

But unfortunately she'd eventually been caught in the act by a raging Brett who wouldn't listen to reason, called her vile names, and told her to get *out, out, out.*

She had nowhere to go but here. So here she was banging on the front door of a twin sister whom she hadn't spoken to in a long, long while.

Her little white Maltipoo, Toto, squirmed uncomfortably in her arms, yapped, and started fidgeting wildly. She let him down quickly, his faux diamond collar glistening in the waning sunlight. Without further ado, the little animal struck an unmistakable pose and quickly did his business right on Lucky's pristine, front sidewalk. Barbara didn't have anything with her to clean it up with, so there the steaming mess had to stay for now. *She'd take care of it later.*

Growing more agitated by the minute, she adjusted the nicotine patch on her upper arm before gathering the tiny dog back up into her arms and tucking him safely into her big carry-all.

Between that patch and the gum, her quitting smoking effort just wasn't working. Maybe she should just rip the itchy thing off of her arm. It didn't seem to do anything except make her more nervous than she already was and maybe now wasn't the right time to try to quit.

Sunset was rapidly approaching and even though this seemed like a good neighborhood, she couldn't stay out here all night. And she was not going to stay in her car.

The Mercedes was twenty years old, the windows worked sporadically, and the poor car was definitely on its last legs. Besides, she had about a fume left for gas and no more money. She was stuck here. *God, she needed a cig.*

Lucky! Where are you?

FEAR AND IMMOBILIZATION

If you've ever found yourself without money, you may have experienced the paralyzing fear that rides along with that. *What do I do now?*

Fear. It's a big one. And it resides in the root chakra. Instead of the primal survival reaction it was originally designed to be, it has now become a PRIMARY vibration, deeply ingrained in our collective consciousness. This is important because it's everywhere. Daily we are fed a seemingly endless diet of fear. There appears to be no escape. Fear is amplified.

With our current advanced technologies, fear is in our faces every day whether or not we want to see it. It's become like its own operating system. We can try to ignore it but such a thing reverberates and intertwines with our very fabric. Fear affects us on all levels.

But we play our part in this drama by "buying" into fear. We seem to be deeply invested in it. Fear is big business, isn't it? How many times have you clicked on a headline or ad on the

Internet that draws you to do so by using fear as the bait? Someone gets paid for your clicking.

And what are you perhaps most afraid of besides dying, perhaps? If you are honest with yourself, it's most probably the fear of having no money and therefore no power. But money is not power. It's energy.

Albert Einstein supposedly said this about energy: "Everything is energy and that's all there is to it. Match the frequency of the reality you want and you cannot help but get that reality. It can be no other way. This is not philosophy. This is physics." And regardless of who said it, they are right, of course.

Everything is energy. *Money* is energy. We can hear those words, and we can read those words, but the truth is that many people aren't even at the halfway point of fully understanding, embracing, or implementing these statements. Instead, money is still perceived as power. That's the ingrained perception.

Profit, numbers, and the "bottom line" have become all important. We still equate money with survival, with perhaps "survival of the fittest," dependent upon how much money we have or can manage to accumulate. But what if it all went away? What if our pieces of paper ceased to have "value?" What if they became like any of the other paper that sits upon your desk? Does that scare you?

Until we learn that these pieces of paper are just the format that we chose long ago in order to exchange with one another, we will never fully understand money as energy.

But if we could do that—start understanding money as energy instead of power—we would cease to have money issues. We would cease to have a lot of issues. Do we need a total monetary collapse to be able to do that? Think about how frightened you may feel about that statement. And what is your natural inclination then? To hoard and stockpile something of "value," such as gold or silver? Paintings? Jewelry or gemstones?

But if we understand "value," and we understand value and money as perceptions, and we know who we are at a root level, money ceases to have power over us and fear dissipates, clearing the pathway ahead. *I am okay everywhere I go and everywhere I am.* When we know who we are, and have confidence in our ability to exchange (I am not talking about barter here), and create our existence from who we really are, *that* becomes primary instead of fear. And thus we open the flow to the energy of money.

It's not that tall of an order if we reduce it to its basic essence. Even if we cannot change the whole paradigm instantaneously, we can start to make a difference in our personal reality at individual levels. Changing things on individual levels has much more power than we might realize. Honoring each other's life force energy in *every* exchange, and honoring our own as well, is a good place to start.

In every interaction—every single one—ask yourself if it honors you or not. I'm not talking about being grateful. That isn't it. Ask if the exchange of energy honors the other party as well. If it doesn't, then ask yourself why you are willing to do whatever it is, why you are willing to engage in anything other than a fair exchange of energy?

And then when you have that, you will have some good answers that have the ability to take you to the root. Again, when we can clear out the root we then open the pipeline to the energy flow of money and more.

GRATITUDE

Gratitude has become very popular. At this writing, there are even "gratitude challenges." Basically, these are where you write down x number of things you are grateful for every day. This is nice and it is good. But again, similar to the way people were taught to manifest by writing themselves a check and then putting a lot of mental focus on it and hoping it would transform into money, this exercise is flat and linear and doesn't really do much. I'm not saying it doesn't do anything or that it isn't good to do. I'm saying it's not operating at full power.

Yes, we have to start somewhere and yes, gratitude is a necessary part of manifesting. And yes, we should indeed be grateful for ALL. It's when gratitude stays flat and linear—just words on a paper—like the check we wrote ourselves, that it ceases to have the power to transform much of anything. In order for gratitude to be *gratitude*, it needs the power of emotion to ride along with it and propel it into the powerful force that it truly is.

It is not enough to say you are grateful, write three things you are grateful for and stare at them all day long, or even share them on social media with ten other people. Gratitude is not something you do. It's something you *are*. Do not "practice" gratitude. Instead, *BE* grateful. Then you will see how gratitude really works in your life.

A TALE OF WOE:
A different perspective on patterns and entitlement

Let's say you are sitting in the middle of the ocean in a small boat. Your boat springs a slow leak. You pray for someone to come and save you. Soon, along comes a larger boat. By this time you are really thirsty.

The people in the larger boat offer to throw you a towline. You are focused on your thirst; so you tell them you are just thirsty and could use some water. *If only you had some water!*

They throw you some ice cold bottled water. You guzzle it down without further ado. They ask again if they can throw you a lifeline. You hesitate in answering. There may be some work involved with this, i.e., you may have to stand up and actually attach the line to your own boat and do a few other things. Plus, you really are afraid of falling out of your boat and maybe even losing your very attractive and expensive sunglasses in the process.

Your thirst quenched for the moment, you politely decline the lifeline, content to wait for someone to save you. They look at you rather dumbfounded, but move along their path.

Pretty soon your slow leak is getting larger and a storm is coming. You pray again for someone to come and save you. Along comes another even larger boat. By this time you are really hungry, and this is a fishing boat on its way in with its big catch of the day. They offer you a lifeline. You see the fruits of their all day labor and you want this for yourself.

You feel entitled to this because, after all, you are in a small, leaky boat and they have a bigger boat. You say rather woefully, "I don't really need a lifeline right now. But if only I had some fish I wouldn't be hungry anymore."

So they throw you some fish, which you quickly gobble up. It's free. It's fresh. And it's good! They again offer you a lifeline.

Your stomach full, you politely decline because now you are a bit too satiated and sleepy to do whatever is required to help tow your boat in. You don't even really care anymore about getting towed in. *That fish was really good!* Your boat seems comfortable enough for now. And eventually someone will come along and save you. They depart.

Your boat soon starts sinking; and while it is going down you wonder why no one showed up to save you. You need a miracle. You go down thinking, as you always have: *This kind of stuff always happens to me.*

* * * * *

What is it with this feeling of entitlement? What is it with the idea that someone is going to save you or that saving you is a "miracle?" This is not a miracle. No one is going to save you. People may offer you assistance, but you have to actually do something to assist yourself as well. Even if you are afraid to reach over and tie the lifeline to your boat, or do whatever else may be necessary to assist in your "saving," it is better to try to do so than to sink and drown, all the while wondering what in the world happened.

There are those that would go down saying to themselves that at least someone thought enough of them to give them basics such as food and water. Did you perhaps forget to think enough of yourself to provide yourself with such? And there are those who would go down blaming someone else for not providing them with swimming lessons.

There are many along the path who are willing to provide you with basics. You may not even appreciate those basics or those foundations—and not be grateful for them—until or unless you have to provide them for yourself. You may not even realize you have been provided with basics on which and with which to build a foundation. But know this: If you are an adult, you are not *entitled* to have anyone else provide them for you. It's just simply true.

Is it necessary to take things in your life to the point where you are actually sitting in a teeny little boat with a hole in it in the middle of the ocean before you realize that you are not entitled to have a bigger, better boat *just because*?

* * * * *

So, to continue our tale. . . Before your boat sinks completely, another even larger boat comes by and the deckhands offer you a towline. You are exhausted by your journey. It's been so hard!

This time you take the offer because you have come to realize the desperateness of your situation. You even manage to tie the rope to your boat all by yourself without falling in. However you do lose your designer sunglasses, and woefully, the money you had in your pockets did fall into the ocean and got washed away. You watch in helpless dismay.

* * * * *

When you safely reach shore, the captain of the larger boat bids you farewell with a wave and a smile. You do not offer to exchange anything with this captain or crew because:

(1) Your money was lost at sea and;
(2) It doesn't occur to you to offer anything.

You feel entitled to be "saved," primarily because you were sinking; and after all, you are the one with the smaller boat.

In any event, you are now safe. You are on your own. You are free from impending doom; but you are not free from your *patterns* yet, as we shall see.

* * * * *

You glance around at your surroundings and you notice an older building with a sign in the window that says: HELP WANTED

Before we get to that however, there are some things you do *not* see because you only have your own limited perspectives:

The larger boat was taking a risk by towing you in. They ended up having to get new engines and repairing some other general damage that occurred by the towing of your boat. The captain also paid his crew overtime for their extra time and effort. You will never come to find this out; and even if you did find out, you would have no intention of doing anything about it (what could you even *do*?) because you wouldn't consider it to be your issue. *The captain can afford to fix these things himself— look at the size of his boat! And his crew is his responsibility, not yours.*

* * * * *

You walk into the building with the "Help Wanted" sign in the window. You are darn thirsty again and you could really use a cigarette after all you've been through. *My God, what an ordeal you've endured!* And you still have the challenge of getting your boat fixed so you can continue on your journey.

The building is a bar/restaurant kind of establishment with a lot of local flavor. *Wonderful!* Come to think of it, you could really use a drink. *How convenient.* But you have no money since all of your pieces of paper got washed away when you helped tie the towrope to your boat.

You sidle up to the bar and pitifully explain your tale of woe to the bartender. You even shed a tear or two for all you've been through. You have found that a little "boo hoo" at the right time goes a long, long way.

Feeling sorry for you as you had hoped, the

bartender pours you a stiff one and says it's on the house. *Excellent! How kind of him.* You gratefully gulp it down. You bum a cigarette from a patron.

The bar is filled with people, and you are hoping someone will take pity upon you and your recent travails and buy you another drink.

No one does, however, even though you are freely and happily relating your tale of woe to whomever is in earshot. You have always understood and enjoyed the language of victim-speak.

But what you fail to realize is that these are fishermen/women. They work, and they work hard. They are victims to nothing and they truly do not understand your language. You may as well have been speaking Swahili.

After relating your tale of woe to many in hope that someone will help you out here, someone mentions that help is wanted at this establishment. They need a dishwasher.

You are utterly astounded at this suggestion. *This work is completely beneath you! You cannot possibly do such a thing!*

You may have a small, leaky boat, but you have an education. You have a Ph.D. You even have five courses of mathematics! You mention this to someone, even though they are not particularly impressed. Theirs is a different world in which pieces of paper as definitions of who you are really do not matter much.

But in *your* "real world" you are a very important person. *No, you cannot even consider such a thing as being a dishwasher!*

* * * * *

Some of the patrons start giving you what you consider to be the "fish eye," and you are growing rather uncomfortable. You decide that you better get out of this place fast before the natives get restless.

You need to find someone willing to help you fix your boat so you can get out of here. You silently curse that captain. *What was he thinking bringing you here to this unfriendly place?*

You exit the bar/restaurant and start walking. You're just sort of meandering around, but you're getting very tired. You see a sign that says:

Spiritual Guru/Healer →This Way

You follow the arrow. *Certainly the healer will help you get out of here*. You walk on an uphill path in the direction of the arrow, thinking to yourself *this healer better be worth the hike.*

You soon come to a clearing and you see a big, beautiful dwelling. You think to yourself that if this is where the spiritual guru's office is, they must be very rich and powerful and certainly in a good position to help you. *For free*, of course.

Isn't "healing" always free? Aren't these people just doing what they are supposed to be doing? Isn't spirituality free? *Yes,* you say to yourself. *Of course it is!*

You come upon a big carved wooden door. This is really ornate. Based upon what you see before you, you reiterate to yourself, *My, this person must be really well compensated.*

You knock on door with the very expensive looking doorknocker. *Hurry up already!*

* * * * *

Let's rewind a little. Sometimes we have to do that in life. We're doing it now because it's important to note in terms of deep seated patterns and belief systems.

So. . .after you left the bar/restaurant, you were followed by a pack of angry looking canines. You thought maybe the patrons in the bar sent them out after you. You are afraid of dogs because as a child you were mauled by one and almost blinded in the process. This has traumatized you for life. You do not like dogs. *Why are these things following you? And curses again on that captain for bringing you here, and on those patrons. They seemed nice at first.* But then they turned on you for no reason.

You walked on nervously and quickly, hoping the angry dogs would just go away. You thought to yourself: *This can't possibly happen again, can it?* But they didn't go away. And the more fearful you became, the more aggressive they seemed to become. You attracted this to you by your fear, but you wouldn't quite put it that way. You just wanted them to leave you alone. But, as I said, they didn't.

And to your horror, you actually did end up getting attacked by these nasty looking creatures. And this is why you are overjoyed, albeit torn, tattered, and bloody, at finally arriving at and knocking loudly on the very ornate and impressive door of the healer. *This person is meant to help you!*

"Open up already! I am wounded!"

Finally, someone shows up. You expected a servant to answer, but the door is answered by the healer himself.

Wow, you think to yourself. *I want whatever this person is having.* You manage to curb a pang of jealousy and hope the healer doesn't notice. *Don't want to get off on the wrong foot here.*

Your wounded gaze is met by the deepest, clearest, most aquamarine eyes you have ever seen. Come to think of it, you don't recall seeing eyes this color ever before. You are temporarily mesmerized. You manage to snap out of it and hastily gather your wits. You don't know what's wrong with you. You normally have legendary cool. *Maybe a spell has been cast upon me,* you think to yourself.

"I'm wounded!" you exclaim again in case the guru didn't hear you yelling when you were outside the door. You look behind you and the nasty dogs have thankfully disappeared.

The healer gazes upon you lovingly and beckons you in. "Ah, yes," he says. "Being one of the keepers of the sacred records, I've been expecting you. You're a little early, but I saw you in my crystal ball not too long ago. Come, I've made you some pancakes."

You'll have pancakes as long as they're free, you think to yourself. Judging by the looks of this place, they can't be free. You have no money, after all. *What does this person expect from you?* You're a little wary and all you want is some assistance and healing. *That has got to be free!*

You cautiously follow along behind the healer, down a long corridor, dripping a conspicuous trail of blood on the white marble floor. You begin to wonder if this person knows what they are doing. They seem a bit daft. The guru hasn't even seemed to notice the dripping blood.

Still, you find yourself strangely attracted or drawn to this person in some odd way. And not in a funny way. It just feels like you've known one another forever. This makes you feel a bit uncomfortable, but you'll go along with it for now. *You need healing!*

You take a seat at an ornately carved alder table. *Impressive.* The healer has disappeared to who knows where. As you wait patiently for your pancakes and maybe a bandage or two, you look around. You notice many crystals, gemstones, and some items you don't recognize. You make a somewhat subconscious note of the gemstones.

The healer comes back into the room and brings you some bandages and tends to your flesh wounds. *Finally!*

Soon after that a plate of steaming pancakes appears on the table, seemingly out of thin air.

You must have lost more blood than you thought. *You're imagining things.* You wolf the pancakes down. *Not bad.* You're extremely hungry and exhausted after your ordeal. *Who wouldn't be? Yes, these are free, you've decided. This guru has more than enough of everything.*

* * * * *

All in all, you spend a total of six months at the house of the healer. The healer tends to your wounds—physical, emotional, and spiritual—and makes you feel better. Physically, you are pain free for the first time in your life. *This is how life is meant to be.*

One day the healer tells you that it is time to embark upon a vision quest. For this you will need to learn to breathe in a certain way. You moan, groan, and complain at the assignment, but you agree to learn it. You practice that breathing endlessly it seems.

Then suddenly the day of travel is upon you. You and the healer go on your trip and you hike for what seems to be forever. After much ado, you end up on a very high bluff. You both sit down and enjoy the ambiance. You feel at peace there. You could stay forever. But you don't really know what you're supposed to be "questing" for.

You hope that not too much work is required. It's not that you're lazy or anything. *You're definitely not lazy.* You've worked and been responsible your whole life. At this point you just like to go with the flow and if it's not easy, you don't want to do it.

As if reading your thoughts, the healer tells you that you are looking for your totem. *Totem? What's a totem?* Suddenly, as if by magic, appears a leopard.

The healer informs you that this is your totem. You seem to get a sense of the truth of that. You are, of course, somewhat intuitive. You accept the leopard totem, in some way, and on some level. But you have no idea what this totem represents or even what a totem is. Nor do you much care, actually, if truth be told. You find that your needs in the moment are being met and that is all that matters to you. *It's so peaceful here* and the Universe knows you definitely needed a vacation.

While you've been here the guru has taken care of your physical pain and most of all your other needs as well. You have an uneasy feeling about the ultimate tab for this experience. But you remind yourself that this is all free. You don't give much deep thought to the leopard and eventually it disappears.

* * * * *

Upon returning from your travels and to the main house, you dream several times about the leopard. You still have no idea what any of that means and you have no cause to delve deeper. You're just going with the flow and are quite happy to do so.

Somewhere along the line it becomes clear that your flesh wounds have been successfully attended to, and spiritually you have gone as far as you are willing or able to go here.

It is clear to you that it is time to move along the path. Because the healer does not feel you have learned all you have come to learn he is sad upon learning of your plans to depart, but also accepts that it is your free will choice. You say your goodbyes to each other, however inept and however untimely.

On your way out, you find a check on a side table near the door. It is made out to you and is drawn on *The First National Bank of Karma*. The amount is for $3,765.00.

So thinking that it belongs to you, primarily because it has your name on it—you don't care what bank it's drawn on as long as it clears—you pocket it. *This will come in handy.*

You walk down the long path to the shore. You do not get attacked by dogs again. The way is smooth and uneventful. You are self-satisfied;

and you take it as a sign, thinking that you have indeed learned something valuable from your time at the house of the healer. You have accomplished much.

You eventually find your boat exactly where you left it. Your trust in the innate goodness of the human race renews. After all, it's been several months. However, you see that the boat still has a hole in it. You idly wonder why some native did not fix it for you in your absence. You check your pockets to see what you could possibly use to plug up the hole. You just want to get back to where you were. You've learned a lot; but you just want to be on your way.

The only thing you have in your pocket is that check. You consider for a few moments. It is the only thing that may get you out of here.

Okay. You decide to use it to try to plug the hole. You crumple it up and push it in there and to your surprise you find that it works. Also to your surprise you see that magically the check turns into a rubbery substance, expands into the hole, and seems to be working quite nicely. *Amazing!*

You shove off back into the ocean, climb into the boat, and are excited to go back to where you came from. You just want to get home. Yes, you learned something. A lot of valuable somethings, in fact, and *it didn't cost you anything at all.*

* * * * *

On your third day at sea, your boat springs a leak. The power of the check has run out or perhaps it has bounced.

You find yourself once again sitting in the middle of the ocean in a boat with a hole in it. A storm is again approaching. The boat is sinking.

Along comes another bigger boat. It is that same captain that originally towed you in. You note that he now has a much bigger boat. *Business must be good.* He asks if you want a tow. You tell him, "Yes," but you do not want to go back to the same place.

He obliges. And you find yourself once again tying the line he throws you to your end of the boat. This time you have nothing to lose. You have absolutely nothing. There is nothing left to fall into the raging sea. *Woe is you!*

But this time things are different. As requested, he does not take you to the same island. He instead invites you onto his boat. You accept, leaving your own small, leaky boat tossing violently in the erratic sea.

You climb aboard and the captain beckons you to his chambers. You think this is a little odd, but you oblige because you're curious. To your utter surprise, inside is . . . a leopard, of all things. You cautiously keep your distance, never quite understanding what the whole leopard thing was about anyway.

Uneasily, you broach the subject. You tell the captain you just want to get home. The captain tells you that you *are* home.

What?! You feel a little angry at this statement. You tell him you do not understand, and you are unwilling to put up with any more drama or nonsense or things you do not understand.

You went through this crazy motion whatever it was all about. In the process you lost your money in the sea; you lost a check for $3,765.00. And you remind him that you lost your designer sunglasses as well. You did everything that was asked or expected of you, did you not?

The captain looks at you with sadness and compassion in his eyes and tries to explain.

"My child," he begins. "The very first time that you chose to refuse help and your boat went down is when you died. You see, death is not even remotely how you imagined it to be.

"When we came along and offered you a tow, you were already gone.

"We took you to a place where you had a chance of life anew. And there *you applied all of your old thinking and all of your old patterns to a new situation.*

"You learned absolutely nothing new, and in fact incurred new karma by taking something that appeared to be yours but was not. In this world things are not always what they seem and the things you thought had value are completely meaningless here.

"You cannot go back. You can only go forward. The leopard is to remind you that leopards do not change their spots. You did not accept the leopard as your totem because you refused to see your unwillingness to change. You refused to see your part in your own incarnation. You refused to take responsibility for any of your choices. That is the meaning of the leopard.

"But, as with anything, one can choose a different animal as a totem at the appropriate time. You and the animal will choose each other.

"Now this incarnation is over, but I will take you to the place where you can start over. You will not remember any of this on a conscious level, but you will have signals and signs and you will meet people that remind you in some way of the life lessons that you are supposed to learn. These people and things will seem vaguely familiar to you.

"You will even encounter another leopard and will again have a choice about whether or not to accept and fully embrace the learning of this totem into your life or not. It is up to you.

"Everything is all up to you. You can also choose, as you had a choice whether or not to accept a towline—and *when*—or to take the check or not, to look at this incarnation as a complete failure or as something that impacts you and others on a universal level. It is your choice whether or not to accept this lifetime as a failure or as a success.

"Those reading your story now may come to understand the role they play in their own tale. They also have the choice as you did as to whether or not their story becomes a tale of woe or not. It is *all* a choice."

And with that, life began anew as it always does.

Do you get it?

THE EGO AND EGO PERCEPTIONS

The ego in its healthy state does have its purpose. The ego self is basically what keeps us here, grounded in this incarnation, doing what we came to do. But our perceptions of ourselves and others can become quite distorted based upon whatever it is we fool ourselves into believing at any particular time. For example, the concept of self-love seems to have evolved into an excuse to be unabashedly narcissistic, self-focused, self-involved, and self-centered.

None of those have anything whatsoever to do with self-love. Self-love has to do with healthy boundaries, honor, and respect for the self; the physical, mental, and emotional spiritual selves.

When examining your perceptions, being honest with yourself is one of the most challenging things to do because it requires that you take an objective viewpoint of yourself *and* your choices. It is much easier for us to see other people's issues than it is for us to see our own. This is one reason why many things we encounter are reflections. This reference, this vantage point, gives us opportunity to view things in a new, different, and hopefully enlightening way.

LUCKY

Lucky returned from the gym and the grocery store right around sunset to find a hooker on her doorstep. Or at least that's what the bleached blonde woman standing on her front porch looked like to her.

She pulled into the driveway, turned the ignition off in her late model SUV, got out and started up the sidewalk. Here she stepped quite unceremoniously into some very new. . . dog poop. *What in the world?*

As she got closer, the picture came more into focus. It was her twin sister. *Good grief*, did *she* look like this?

"Barbie! What are you doing here?" Lucky exclaimed. *And what in the world are you wearing?* she thought to herself, yet didn't say it aloud. The bling was overdone to the point of being blinding, even in the quickly fading sunlight. The tight jet black halter top accentuated Barbie's long, shiny blonde hair and the amount of cleavage showing through the thin fabric was. . .well. . .it definitely left nothing to the imagination. The even tighter short shorts were definitely way too short. And . . .*Enough*, Lucky thought. She'd better stop gaping and try to find out what Babs was doing here.

"Hi Sis!" Barbie exclaimed, jumping excitedly up and down a little like a child might do. "I came for a visit!" Lucky noticed oddly that nothing jiggled. Nothing.

Stunned, or momentarily blinded by the bling, *or something,* Lucky managed a terse, "Hello, Sis!" Fumbling with the key in the front door Lucky managed a slightly muffled, "Come on in."

Toto, the tiny white dog, poked his head out from inside the tote and gave a little yap in the way of greeting. *Well, that certainly explained the poop. Why hadn't Barbie cleaned it up?*

The two twins hadn't seen or spoken to each other in years. Lucky had loaned Barbara some money back then, a lot of money, and she had never gotten paid back. It hadn't been a gift, it was clearly a loan, and Lucky hadn't been in any kind of solid monetary position herself at that time to do such a thing. But it was family, it was her *twin*, for goodness sake, and so she had done what she thought was the right thing at the time.

However, it had been years, and Barbie had just taken the money as if it were her due, and gone off again with one of her boyfriends of the moment to who knows where. Lucky hadn't heard anything from Barbara since. And that had been a long time ago now. Not a phone call, letter, email, nothing in all this time. To find Barbie on her doorstep now could only mean one thing. *Trouble*.

* * * * *

Once inside and the lights on, Lucky said, "We'll catch up in a minute, Babs. I need to go out to the car to get the groceries."

"Okay," was her sister's reply. No offer of help. Barbie had already made herself comfortable on the soft, cocoa brown sectional.

Exasperated already, and rolling her eyes, Lucky replied, "Okay." And out she went reminding herself not to step again in the poop.

BARBARA

Barbie was ultra-sensitive but it didn't take a psychic to figure out that Lucky thought she was here to freeload. But that wasn't it. Barbie just needed some support. So when Lucky finished bringing the groceries in, Barbie got up from the couch and helped her put them away. Besides, she was extremely hungry and wanted to see what was available for grub.

Barbie was a lot of things, but one of her more useful talents was gourmet cooking. Give her a bunch of ingredients, and even if there wasn't much there, she could always manage to make something quite extraordinary out of almost nothing.

Unbelievable, probably, given the way she looked on the outside, but she was actually quite good at it. It seemed to be a special, innate talent.

No one had taught her how to cook or bake. She just knew how. Food was survival, after all, and Barbie's opinion of her journey was that it was so hard and so challenging. . . well . . .she was an expert at survival. *And thank God she had a fast metabolism.*

Her particular specialty was making things out of dough, like batter, muffins, and bread.

Anything she made out of dough always seemed to rise up and transform into something quite magical.

Barbie quickly surveyed the groceries Lucky had brought home and determined she had enough of everything needed to make her special mini seafood quiche muffins. So she did. . .

Mini Seafood Quiche

Makes 12 tasty little treats

1 puff pastry sheet, rolled out, or puff pastry shells. (Find it in the frozen "novelties" section of your grocery store)

1/2 cup shredded Italian four or six cheese blend
1/2 cup crabmeat or imitation crabmeat, thawed and ready to use
9 or more shrimp, cooked, tail removed, and cut into pieces
1/2 cup canned artichoke hearts, drained and cut into pieces
Onion powder
Seafood spice blend
Hot spice, hot sauce, or hot paprika as desired
Parsley, chopped
Salt and pepper
Grated Parmesan cheese, sprinkle
3 eggs
1-1/2 cups heavy whipping cream

Preheat oven to 425 degrees. Thaw puff pastry sheet. Roll out to approximately 12" x 14" on lightly floured surface. Unless using puff pastry shells, cut the dough with cup, glass, cookie cutter, or knife into 12 round circles with a 3-3/4" diameter. Fit and snuggle the pastry into standard muffin pan cups. Sprinkle bottoms evenly with shredded cheese.

Cut the seafood and artichokes into small pieces. Place in small bowl. Stir in the spices, seasonings and Parmesan cheese. Spoon evenly into pastry cups.

In another bowl, with a wire whisk, beat eggs with cream. Pour over seafood in cups to full.

Sprinkle with more Parmesan. Bake 15 minutes. Reduce the heat to 300 degrees. Bake 20 to 30 minutes longer or until egg mixture is done, golden brown and puffed. *Instead of seafood, fill the mini quiches with any vegetables or combination of meats and vegetables that you enjoy.*

* * * * *

Much like the delectable little quiches, Barbie and Lucky kept the dinner conversation as light as the accompanying Pinot Blanc. They even had a few laughs.

As light as the food and wine was, after dinner, Lucky told Barbie they needed to have a serious talk. Lucky being Lucky, just jumped right in and stated rather bluntly, "I'm really happy to see you, Sis, but please know that I can't support you, Barbie. I've been renting out this house and the little casita now for the past few years. If I didn't need the income, I wouldn't rent these out at all. But I do, so I do."

Barbie just stared at her, rather vacantly it seemed, like a deer in the headlights, not saying anything.

The non-response was a little unnerving and Lucky wasn't quite sure what to make of it.

She paused a moment and then continued, blue eyes meeting blue eyes in a steady, level gaze. "You can stay in the casita but I need you to pay rent, pull your own weight. I'm doing okay. But again, I'm not in a position to support you. And I can't pay for your utilities either. You'll have to pay for what you use in that regard. If you're going to stay, you're just going to have to get a job."

Barbara slowly nodded and said she understood. She would try her best to honor the agreement. *She would find psychic work in the morning.*

WHAT DOES FOOD AND COOKING HAVE TO DO WITH MONEY?

Did you ever notice that very wealthy people often hire other people to cook for them? Why? Part of this is a function of time. Part of it is a root chakra value system. Food is survival. Sometimes we equate food to love. Sometimes we equate being waited on, being served our food, as our due or something we "deserve."

Sometimes we perceive that when someone else makes our food, it just tastes better or it is better. For some, there is some kind of value equated with someone else making the food. But however you slice the cake, or how many fancy frostings you put on it, food is simply very root chakra and basic.

In any kind of cooking or baking, we are starting with raw ingredients and then creating a finished product from those. We're essentially transforming energy.

It's fundamentally the same process to create money. You take the raw ingredients of your root chakra drive and ambition, combine these with your gifts and talents, and transform them into the energy that comes back around and sustains you. You make a living.

We do not have to cook or bake to be able to make money, create money, or make a living. But since food is so root chakra, and money is too, it is wise to have a good look at and examine from what and from where you are being "fed," and what and from where you *expect* to be fed. And as well, and most importantly, examine what it is you are feeding yourself.

PATTERN: SELF SABOTAGE

Self-sabotage occurs in several different ways and on several different levels. For example, sometimes someone brings you a message, but you're not ready or open to receive it and do not want to receive it because whatever you're doing at the moment works for you.

As well, we should note that everything speaks whether or not we are listening at any given moment. The universe is always humming, speaking, communicating. But if you aren't receptive to the message or messages, for whatever reasons, your ego self will make up all manner of excuses as to why you can't or shouldn't implement whatever the messenger tells you.

So now what has happened is that you've blocked your pathway for receiving. The more you stay stuck in what the ego thinks it should do or not do, the more you stay entrenched in your patterns, the more stuck you stay. And there you spin your wheels around and around and around in an endless circle.

Until you can hear what's being said, until you can absorb what's being told to you, then integrate, and implement whatever it is, you cannot move forward out of the muck. You can only move laterally, if at all. And all the while you keep spinning a deeper hole.

We can sometimes see ourselves sinking and recognize that we are sinking, however, if the current pattern is working in some way, we will tend to stay with that pattern because it's what we know or it is what seems easiest. This is the ego self leading us rather than us leading it.

We've all seen this happen. A parent tells a child or teenager "no," and the child does whatever it wants to do anyway. Why? It's because the ego self is in command and engaged in a power struggle with its "higher self," while at the same time trying to "find oneself."

There is resistance to being integrated with our higher self because we may perceive integration to be hard, or we may have to change, or change may require some effort. The ego will always try to take the path of least resistance and will always fool itself into thinking it is right in almost any situation. The ego will present with excuses that seem perfectly valid to the intellect of the mind.

Everyone learns in their own way and in their own time. So people can tell you something and you may not believe it until you experience whatever it is for yourself. And as well, it may take several times of repeating the same behavior in order for the body and mind to register it and process it in the emotional body as bad, harmful, self-destructive, or just plain non-productive.

Now let's say, for example, that you need to get a job. But you're older and all of your friends are retiring now. You have some basic resistance, therefore, to having to get a job, even though you aren't totally adverse to the concept of "work." You don't view yourself as lazy. You just feel as if you should be at a different level in life at this point. But you're not. So you then perhaps go about trying to "create from who you are," and you find that nothing works. This is perplexing to you.

What you must do in this situation, to get off of "square one," is to get to the root. And that's where people sometimes get stuck. It does take some work to get to the root, to face what's there, and then to actually do something about it.

First of all you must get yourself out of the initial perception that just because everyone else you know is retiring, that you should be able to do so as well. What someone else does or doesn't do does has nothing to do with you.

To free yourself from this generalized perception of the ego, you must first examine all of the choices you've made in life that have brought you to wherever you are now. Then take responsibility for them.

Examine why you may have this perception, whatever it is. Where did it originate from? And then just get over it. . . all of it. Jump over it if you have to, because that big barreled, ego based perception is right in the way of you moving forward.

Then next, in order to move forward, you must move yourself to a position of power rather than allowing yourself to stay stuck in the crumbling abode of victimhood. But that too is a choice. Choose to examine your underlying belief systems.

Do you believe the Universe will save you, God will save you, *the healer or guru will save you?* Or do you believe there is no saving necessary?

Almost everyone will encounter some kind of spiritual or financial crises somewhere on their journey, and some people's journeys are more challenging than others because that is what they chose as a platform and stage for working out their dramas.

It's when you make a career out of "victim mode," that you've got a big problem. When you're a "victim" you are engaging in self-sabotage and possibly manipulation.

To propel yourself out of this mode, and thus move forward, first ask yourself what you do with what's been provided to you, what you do with the messages that come your way, the signs that show up, the tools that are given to you, the natural gifts and talents that you have, the time that you have? *What do you do with these things?* In what ways do you honor all that has been provided for you?

REPEATING PATTERNS: A FORM OF SELF-SABOTAGE

At the point where we aren't listening to the messages that come our way, not honoring much of anything, including ourselves, or just find ourselves generally stuck, the natural tendency is to repeat our patterns. This truly doesn't make much sense if you think about it, because those patterns are usually what got us stuck in the first place. And repeating them will keep us right where we are, sometimes for years.

But when we're stuck, we can get scared and immobilized. And when we're scared, we tend to operate from that primal place, the root. And we tend therefore to do what is familiar to us. . .our patterns.

So whatever is deeply ingrained in the root, is what we will find ourselves doing, gravitating toward, and *attracting*. That's why it's important to examine all of the patterns and energies that reside there within you at the root, and then clear out what just doesn't do you any good or help move you forward on your path.

To get unstuck, we have to *change the vibration and the frequency of a pattern that is keeping us stuck. And we have to do that at the root*. That's when the Law of Attraction comes into play. And when we change this *frequency*, that's when we find that we attract something else as if by magic. But nothing can meet you and go forward with you on the path if you're standing there blocking the way.

Let's say for example, that you are a teacher. You've spent your life teaching and it's what you know. You don't love the profession, but it's your comfort zone. You may believe it to be who you are, what you're supposed to do, and it has always brought you a good living. But now the school district you work for is experiencing budget cuts and you suddenly and unexpectedly get laid off.

Your first reaction to this news is fear. You have just bought a new house and have a hefty mortgage to pay. You do have a small 401K but no other savings, as you just lived from paycheck to paycheck for years, never really giving much thought to the future.

You are able to collect your wits, however, and figure you will just be able to get another teaching job somewhere else. The fear subsides momentarily and you are able to focus on and spend some productive time at home polishing your resume and doing all you can to do get yourself and your teaching skills out there and on the market. Certainly you will just get another teaching job soon.

After six months nothing has happened in this direction, you still do not have another job, and you're starting to panic. You are not to the point yet where you will subjugate yourself to engaging in work that you consider beneath you, but in your nightmares you can envision that time fast approaching.

Meanwhile, a friend is getting rid of a piano, just giving it away, and asks if you want it. You agree. You've played the piano since you were very young, and although you haven't played in years, you wouldn't mind having the piano. Besides, you have the space and the piano is free. So why not?

A few days after the piano arrives, another friend tells you that a certain band is looking for a new piano player. It doesn't even remotely dawn on you that this could be you.

You don't know why your friend is even telling you this as it has nothing to do with you. You are a teacher.

Your perception is that all musicians are "starving artists." This perception is why you didn't previously pursue a career in music, even though one of your degrees is in music. *Playing the piano is enjoyable, but it's certainly no way to make a living. Besides,* you remind yourself again, *you haven't played in years.*

A few weeks later, your teaching job hunt still in full swing, you finally have an interview. You believe it goes well. At the end of the interview, the interviewer mentions—oddly, you think—that his son is in a band that is looking for a piano player. He asks you if you know of anyone. You tell him you don't. Again, you don't know why this person is asking you this.

You ultimately don't get that particular teaching job, for what reasons you are not sure. But now you are starting to get depressed. You just don't understand the Universe at all or what it expects you to do.

Soon thereafter, you begin engaging in some very old patterns of behavior just to make yourself feel better. These things always worked before whenever you needed some soothing, so you expect them to do so now.

It doesn't matter what these are, whether they are drinking, smoking, drug use, promiscuous behavior, shopping, shoplifting, or yelling at the dog. Whatever they are, they don't do anything to move you forward.

What moves you forward is paying attention to the messages you're receiving—however odd they seem to you—and being willing to do something about them, rather than insisting on going in the directions that your ego self tells you to go.

When we're stuck, we need to try to tune into our innate higher guidance—that we all possess—and be willing to let go of the way we *think* our lives should show up. We need to get to the very root of who we are. And sometimes the root is buried under a lot of years of ingrained perception.

Now, for example, what you may not be seeing here in this situation is that the Universe doesn't necessarily want you to become a piano player in a band. Have you ever heard a song on the radio that you haven't heard in a long time and suddenly you are transported as if by magic back to those very emotions you felt when that song was at the height of its popularity? Music works on an emotional body level to help us get unstuck. Music and sound waves are vibration and frequency. We don't process music with our linear minds.

So what if, instead of spinning around in fear mode, or staying stuck in ego mode going in the direction the linear mind tells you to go, you allowed yourself to invest instead in the messages that are being brought forth? If you did that you might then suspend the job hunt for a little while—just let go, as you are fine for right now—and go in the direction that you were being pointed, however nonsensical it may seem to you at the time.

So let's say you did that, and you simply took a few weeks off from the intensely focused job hunt and played your piano every day for hours instead, reconnected with it and the music that is most assuredly inside you and still part of who you are, however dormant.

Whether you understand it consciously or not, that's the direction where you were being pointed. It takes some degree of trust to follow those arrows, especially when we have the ego persistently yammering at us to do something else; to do what we already know.

But after doing this, allowing yourself to—however reluctantly—follow these messages, to your stunned surprise, a few weeks later you receive a phone call regarding a teaching job.

It's not a regular teaching job like you had before. This job is special and different. And it's an amazing opportunity. It's teaching music to musically gifted autistic children at a private school. The pay scale and benefits are way more than you ever received from any of your previous teaching jobs.

You accept! That Universe may know what it's doing after all. All you had to do was be willing to follow the guidance presented, even if you didn't understand at the time the reasons why it was being presented.

PERCEPTIONS OF VALUE

In the belief systems we have set up for ourselves, the mind tells us that when something is scarce, it is then more valuable. But is that necessarily true? Why not honor things while they are here? Why does scarcity necessarily create a system of value?

We don't honor things or people while they are in front of us because we take them for granted. Take that in, because that is the only answer to why we don't honor everything that shows up in our lives. We believe they or it will always be here. Hence our utter shock or surprise when something or someone ceases to exist.

With money, we don't often think of money supply, per se. Most people don't think in these kinds of economic terms every day. We don't think about what the government is doing in terms of money supply.

What we do think about in terms of money supply is how it shows up in our daily lives. We do think about the price of gasoline and the price of groceries and utilities and the like. We think about things that affect our daily survival. But we don't think about these necessarily in a bigger picture. We go to the gas station and get gas. We go to the grocery store and get groceries. Who is thinking about the underlying economics of this? Some are. Most aren't.

But the bottom line is that if there is a gas shortage or a citrus shortage or a cow shortage, we're all paying the price at the pump and at the store. That is what we pay attention to.

Now in our perceptions of value, what do we do with this information and these messages? Do we stockpile these items that we have been led to believe are scarce? That seems to be most everyone's natural inclination and natural reaction.

The point is that if we didn't have these underlying perceptions of value and scarcity, we wouldn't feel the need to stockpile anything, either valuable or scarce. And we may then just find ourselves honoring all and focusing on our ability to create for ourselves from who we are and exactly what it is we need.

ATTITUDES TOWARD "FREE"

If you are a "light worker" and find yourself unable or even unwilling to make money from your spiritual work, first ask yourself at the base, what is your perception of "free?" Were you taught straight out of the gate, or somewhere along the line, that spirituality is supposed to be free?

If you can't get past the idea that spirituality is supposed to be free, you're going to have some challenges making money in this arena. So examine your perceptions at the root regarding "free." Then eliminate them. Ask yourself if you *really* believe that perception about "free" to be true.

Next, remove the ego and its perceptions from the equation. In other words don't ask "Why me? Why do I have such gifts?" It's all just very simple: Those that are here at this time with "light worker" gifts are those who chose to come here to help humanity "grow up" during these very challenging times. You chose it. It was agreed upon before you got here. That's it. That's all. Now *you* need to grow up.

You can also choose to not use your gifts if you'd like. But all in all, you can't get away from who you are, so those gifts are going to bubble up to the surface regardless. From there it is your choice as to what you do with them or not do with them, "Mr. Phelps." But the good news is that it's not "Mission Impossible." And there is no bad news. You're here at a time where all things are possible. Try to embrace these truths, get out of your own way, and just get on with things.

* * * * *

Do spiritual people charge for their gifts or for their time? We all get paid in some manner for our time and for our talents. It's why we have the system we have. *Go to work for yourself or for someone else and come out of it with a paycheck.* That's the way the model works here. Spiritual people making a living (or trying to make a living) in the healing arts are not excluded from that model.

But spirituality and our perception of it has never been high on our list of "valued" professions such as law or medicine. "Light workers," consequently have been low man on the totem pole for years—many shamed for their gifts, told they were evil—and so many shoved their natural gifts down deep inside and pretended it wasn't so.

That is changing now, attitudes are changing, but there are still multitudes of people who firmly believe that the use of spiritual gifts to help others is supposed to be free. It's a deeply ingrained belief system. But it's simply not true.

There is more value in spiritual gifts than there is in some of our most highly regarded, highly compensated positions. We just choose not to see it that way because our perceptions of value are skewed. And many times we simply do not want to face the truth.

* * * * *

SPIRITUALITY AND SPIRITUAL GUIDANCE

We don't follow our innate spiritual guidance for one reason and one reason only. That is that we are entrenched in our root chakra and its illusions; convinced perhaps that spirituality is something we *do* rather than something we *are* or something that is a part of us.

Accessing our spiritual guidance we may believe is something only psychics can do. Not true. We practice spirituality, we practice yoga, we practice gratitude. We are "spiritual" when convenient. But when we do this, "practice" these things, we are missing the point.

We are who we are at the root, and the old adage still stands that leopards do not change their spots. This does not mean that we cannot change our lives. We can, indeed. But we cannot effect these changes by trying to "get" spiritual."

Have you ever known someone who had a very tough life and then suddenly "got religion?" Neither religion nor spirituality is meant to be something we try on at the store, buy, and then take home and wear or show off.

Just like a sweater or a suit, or even a hat, religion and spirituality are not functions of the exterior, not something to be donned when convenient, even if they seem like good or fashionable items to clothe ourselves in. These reside inside of us. By wearing something on the outside, we cannot force our insides to adopt the fabric, integrate the cloth.

Our minds may know and recognize many spiritual or religious truths. But until we integrate these truths on the inside, they cannot be what they are intended to be on the outside, and will remain just as they are—outer clothing on the illusion of the physical body. The body is illusory. The spirit is not. The body is cloaked and clothed. The spirit is only housed. And the spirit only truly hides from the ego.

BARBARA

Barbie, as promised, albeit three days later, had spent the greater part of the day looking for psychic work. She had stopped into more than a few bookstores and shops asking if they wanted or needed psychic readers there. None did. She had even stopped in Carla's Tarot Dream.

The owner of the quaint and popular shop, Carla, who quickly recovered her composure after mistaking Barbie at first for Lucky, agreed to interview Barbara, along with a test reading, and made note of her qualifications. In Carla's world twins were a very lucky omen.

But, Carla told her politely that she had just hired an astrologer, wanted to see how that went first, and didn't need any more readers just then. But she would keep Barbie in mind for when she needed more readers. Barbie said she understood and told Carla that would be fine. They would do the reading and interview anyway and wait for a possible opening.

They both sat down at a nearby table and began the interview and reading. Before the Tarot reading itself, Barbie gave Carla a brief history of her near death experience and how she had then awakened to her psychic abilities and had taught herself how to read the Tarot.

Barbie was a good enough Tarot card reader, and presented the reading with a certain attitude of confidence and authority. So that was good. But in Carla's estimation the woman either avoided the truth, didn't thoroughly know or understand the messages of the cards, or sugar coated her interpretations,

Because she, Carla, of course, knew definitively that the Five of Pentacles, crossed by the Death card, followed by the Tower card was just not a good thing. *Not at all.*

But Barbie glossed over these cards, preferring to focus on the positive aspects of the reading, of which there were many. *What did Carla expect? Should she scare a client to death?*

Imperceptibly dismayed, but dismayed nonetheless, and somewhat shaken by the cards that showed up, Carla managed to keep an outward façade of composure. She thanked Barbie genuinely for her time and talents. Barbie gathered her cards up quickly off the table, gave Carla a warm hug, thanked her for her consideration, and exited the store.

Dejected, from a day spent accomplishing nothing, Barbie put the key into the ignition of the old Mercedes and turned it, only to have nothing happen. *Nothing.* The car was dead. *What else?* she thought to herself. *Why not?* It was perfect icing on the bitter cake of nothing.

Well, at least she was trying. Lucky would just have to deal with that.

Her cell phone battery also dead, she just decided to hitchhike back to Lucky's. And that's when she'd met Frank. He'd picked her up almost right away. The mutual attraction was palatable and immediate and he seemed familiar in some odd way, like it was fate or destiny even.

Even from his sitting position in the expensive, exotic looking sports car, she could tell he was tall and broad, and seemed to be in superior physical shape. She got in the car.

Dark hair and mesmerizing chocolate eyes made the decision easy to say "Y*es*" to his invitation to go get some drinks. And it wasn't as if she had anything better to do. She'd done enough work for the day and she deserved to relax.

As well, in her book drinking was a way to "invoke spirits." She definitely needed to do that as her innate intuition seemed to have momentarily departed.

* * * * *

One drink led to many in the lush, loud, tropical themed bar and before long, she was rather sloshed. She agreed without hesitation to go with him to his rented house up in the canyon. *No problem. May as well have some fun.*

FRANKIE

There was something oddly familiar about this girl, Frankie thought to himself. But he couldn't quite place it. No matter. He had gotten her into bed quite easily and that's all he cared about.

The deed done several times, and hours later, he just wished to be rid of her, but she was rambling on about her life, some of her past relationships, and even her missing child. *Jesus! This was just too much information.*

She suddenly stopped babbling momentarily and stared at him, china blue eyes open wide.

"What?" he asked.

"What do you do for a living?

"I'm an accountant."

"An *accountant?* I never would have figured you for that. Plus I didn't realize accountants made so much money. That's quite a fancy car you have."

Clearly uncomfortable, he mumbled, "Yeah, I do alright for myself," and quickly changed the subject, giving her a look that let her know it was time to go.

Barbie knew all too well this look, and quickly collected her things. Besides, she was glad to go. There was something really unsettling about this house even if it was in an area filled with mansions and considered "old money." And even though the name of the house was *Villa di Luce*, Villa of Light, it very literally gave her the creeps.

* * * * *

Expertly maneuvering the sports car through the winding curves and on down the canyon, Frankie drove Barbie home to Lucky's. Giving her a quick kiss on her cheek he said he'd call.

They always say that. But no one was allowed to make her feel "less than." Not ever. Barbie pouted a little and got out of the car, making sure he got one last clear view of her shapely, taught behind as she made her way to the casita in back of the main house.

But she wasn't worried. She knew she would see this one again. After all, she was as good in the bedroom as she was in the kitchen, maybe even better. And they seemed to have some kind of strange, unspoken, and as of yet unexplored deeper connection. She turned momentarily and watched him back out of the driveway and pull away.

WHAT'S WRONG WITH THE LAW OF ATTRACTION?

Nothing is wrong with the Law of Attraction. We need it. But it's for attracting, not for manifesting or co-creating.

It was taught to millions of people incorrectly as a way to "get what you want." The truth is that the Law of Attraction is but one dot in your bigger picture.

You can put all the mental energy you want on how your picture should look. However, eventually you're going to have to do what is necessary to sketch it out, connect each dot, and then color it in.

The Law of Attraction is a universal law that was recently re-introduced into collective consciousness. But the interesting paradox, if you choose to see it that way, is that it was brought forth backward and distorted, therefore leaving much disillusionment in its wake. We can't move forward at the same time we are going backward.

So we must now "unlearn" the way the Law of Attraction was recently taught and learn how to implement it. And we have resistance to that because we still want what we want. How many of you still believe that you should visualize a check in the amount of money that you want, put a lot of energy on it, and that it will simply show up? Again, this mental part is only *part* of the process. It's not the entire process. And engaging in this behavior creates limitation.

We manifest and co-create from *I AM*—which is the present moment, the NOW—not from the place of *I WANT*. To try to manifest from I WANT is to intrinsically create a space of lack and limitation and more of the same pattern. We set ourselves up then to attract more of that same pattern.

CREATING YOUR LIFE FROM WHO YOU ARE: WHAT'S IN THE WAY?

You are. I know you don't want to hear that. But if you're not creating your life from who you are, and from alignment of mind, body, spirit, plus Universal Spirit, then you and fear are co-creating partners. So examine how well that relationship is going for you. In fact, examine all of your relationships, particularly your relationship with money, because that is a relationship just like any other. And because the energy of money lives in your root chakra, your relationship with money is a primary relationship.

Yes, there are times when we all need to do whatever we need to do momentarily in terms of a job. That's fine, and mostly based upon our previous choices. But if as a long term choice, you're doing something that you don't want to be doing, particularly in the job or career area, look at where and why you are afraid of being who you really are.

Examine where you say things, for example, like: "I'm only working at this job because I need the money, I need the stability, and I need to pay the bills. Someday I will do the work that I really enjoy doing."

What you're telling the universe in that scenario is that you do not believe in your ability to create and co-create from who you are. You are telling the universe that you don't believe in yourself and you don't believe in it. And the universe will reflect back to you exactly what you send out to it. That is the beauty of the Law of Attraction. Following are are a few things you can do to counteract:

THREE THINGS YOU CAN DO NOW TO START COMING INTO ALIGNMENT:

1. Eliminate fear. We cannot create anything from fear except more fear.

2. Get out of your linear mind and examine instead who you are at the root.

3. Ask "What is the next single thing for me to do?" This keeps you in the "right now," which is the space from which all creation begins.

BARBARA

Barbie didn't know exactly why she had told Frankie anything about herself at all, much less tell him about her stolen child. She never talked about it, not even to Lucky.

She was outrageously attracted to Frankie. And it was if something had just compelled her to tell him. Very odd, she thought, because even though her child was missing, and had been now for years, she could have sworn her daughter was still alive. So she didn't think it was her daughter's departed spirit prompting her. *Maybe there were real spirits in that very creepy house*. Barbie shuddered.

Barbie's ex-husband, Anthony, the father of her child, had stolen the baby, Francesca, from her several years ago. That's what the money she had borrowed from Lucky was for even if Lucky didn't know it. It was for an attorney.

No, Lucky didn't know the half of what Barbie had been through. And Barbie had long ago grown tired of what she perceived to be Lucky's judgments about how she lived her life. *We can't all have a rich and famous boyfriend.*

Yes, she had heard about Lucky dating Nicholas. Lucky probably thought that was why Barbie had shown up. . .money. But that wasn't it. Barbie just needed some support at the moment. She needed her family; people who were supposed to love her unconditionally.

Barbie and Anthony had been involved in a bitter, expensive custody lawsuit and Barbie had finally won. But shortly thereafter, Anthony had kidnapped the baby girl from a day care center. Exactly how this had happened, no one seemed to know. No one had any answers. But it had happened. It most definitely had.

She had been overjoyed to find herself pregnant—she wasn't the most fertile of women—and that baby had been the love of her life. But Anthony was physically abusive, and after a very short time, she knew she and the baby had to get away from him. He hadn't liked that idea at all, and repeatedly tried to beat her into submission. He had even tried to kill her more than once. Yes, she had to get away.

And get away she did, setting up a nice, stable, new life for herself and the child elsewhere. But apparently nowhere was far enough away.

Somehow, Anthony tracked her down and the trouble started all over again. He was a bad man, that Anthony. But he *knew* people and Barbie was scared of him. He had taken the baby girl and totally disappeared off the grid.

It seemed at this point that even the FBI had given up. No one could find this man or her daughter, and even though it felt like just yesterday to Barbie, many years had passed from that awful, horrible day when she felt her very soul had been stolen and ripped away from her. At this juncture, she wasn't quite sure even she would recognize her daughter if she saw her. Children grew and changed so quickly. And she didn't even know if she was really still married or not because she didn't know if Anthony was dead or alive.

Really, how in this day and age did people just disappear? It was beyond her how something like this could have happened, and the continual ache in her heart and in her seemingly perpetually empty womb felt completely unbearable at times. There was a hole in her very soul.

Why she had trusted a total stranger with part of this deep, dark piece of her past, she didn't know. But she had and that was that. She couldn't take it back, and besides, she wasn't sure that he had even been listening. Maybe. Maybe not. *What difference did it make anyway?* Maybe it was just easier in some way to talk to someone we didn't know. It was definitely easy to sleep with them.

FRANKIE

Frank was an extraordinarily handsome and charming man, and he knew it. The thin veneer of his classic, charismatic, Sicilian looks, barely covered an intrinsic, interior darkness. But these looks had opened many doors in life that would have otherwise been closed to him. And he had used them to manipulate and maneuver his way through many a situation.

But as good looking as he was, Frankie was a criminal at heart. He, however, didn't see it that way. He fancied himself as a unique kind of character, a pirate of sorts, smooth and charming, on the outside, and yet on the inside completely ruthless. He was willing to do whatever it took to get whatever he wanted.

He robbed from the rich and gave to himself. He thoroughly enjoyed the manipulation game. He enjoyed outsmarting people. It was easy. *People were so stupid.*

And he wasn't just a regular old accountant. He was a forensic accountant. Frankie was also a talented, albeit frustrated, musician. He definitely had the music in him; a completely natural gift. He could play a variety of instruments and he'd never had any formal lessons.

Frankie had the beat, but he could never quite seem to hook up with the right person or people that could further his music career. He had gotten very close, but nothing big had ever transpired.

Maybe it was this back burner frustration that drove him to his criminal ways. Maybe it was something else. He didn't know and didn't much care. He always got what he needed. He knew how to do that and was indeed very good at it.

He hadn't known his father, also a musician—a horn player apparently—from what he had heard, who had left his mother shortly before he was born. But he didn't care about that either. No circumstance could make him feel "less than." None. He had a very good sense of who he was, even if that was a thief or a very cool pirate.

In childhood he'd spent a lot of time with his numerous cousins, and their cousins, and *their* cousins, so he had never been lonely while his mother was at work.

He was highly intelligent and he'd soaked up like a sponge everything that was taught to him, particularly anything that had to do with thievery. He had grown up rough and tough inside and outside, and all in all that's how he liked things. Women were insanely attracted to him, to that dark dangerousness that they sensed lurked just below the surface. And this he enjoyed immensely. *Who wouldn't?*

Still, it wasn't as if he didn't have any feelings. He did. As fluffy and scattered as she seemed, he'd felt almost an instant kinship with this Barbie for some inexplicable reason. It was an odd emotion, and one he wasn't used to nor was it one he could define. Nor did he have any interest in exploring it further. He wasn't about to let her get under his skin. He couldn't afford that.

Frankie had other, more important things to focus on at the moment. One of those things was to figure out how he was going to successfully fleece money out of one very important, ultra-wealthy, and well known person, Mr. Nicholas Fortuna.

Not so long ago Frankie had been highly recommended to Nicholas by that queer little Feng Shui man, Bobby Dubois. There was no other way to get one's foot inside such a wealthy door. A trusted referral was required.

Frankie had done some previous and ongoing accounting work for Dubois, but the guy didn't have the kind of big dough Frankie was interested in. So even though it would have been like taking candy from a baby, he hadn't embezzled anything there. Besides, he enjoyed the thrill of a challenge and there just wasn't one there. It would have been too easy. He'd instead wisely used that situation to springboard himself over to the really big pool of money.

And so here it was. The opportunity of a lifetime. He knew he'd have to be very careful and he had always been careful. He hadn't actually stolen anything from Nicholas yet. He was setting it all up now. But he might have to consider eventually getting rid of the guy's nosy attorney, Carlos something or other, who had been sniffing around as of late. Well, Frankie couldn't say that exactly, but whatever you called it, the radar was up. *Didn't matter.* Frankie was not only well endowed, he was also well connected in all the right places. If and when the time came, he would do whatever needed to be done.

Besides which, Frank was a very smart cookie, and there was no way he was going to ever get caught being as technologically savvy as he was. He'd been doing this for a long time, was very proficient at covering his tracks, and simply moved on to the next unsuspecting victim when the time was right or when the heat seemed like it was going to get too hot.

Consequently, he had money stashed offshore, and he had a multitude of rock solid investments that no one could touch. He'd also had money in Switzerland before he had to get it out of there in a hurry due to new laws that had recently gone into effect. And he even had managed to buy his own private little island. He was very good with money, even if it was other people's money to begin with. It was his now.

His real passion was actually for precious gemstones and jewelry. These had real value. But even though they carried well and were easy to hide, those could be really hard to get rid of. So instead he hoarded and stockpiled them. He knew their value would only continue to rise over the years. For now he enjoyed looking at them, touching them. He loved bling, especially when it was real.

These super rich people, they were really something. They didn't seem to have a clue about money, really. They just raked it in almost unconsciously it seemed—and in many circumstances left the door wide open to being stolen from. It was like they were asking for it. *Idiots, they were, most of them*. *Stupid people just deserved whatever they got.*

YOUR LIFE'S PURPOSE

We all have clues along the way as to what we came to do here. And we have those clues very early on. Whether or not we do what we came to do is determined by the choices we make along the way. Even if you are not encouraged in this direction in life, you always have a choice to follow your own intuition and individual path.

More often than not we meander far off of our original purpose and find ourselves "lost at sea," with a tale of woe, or entrenched in entitlement. You can't really get to your life's purpose if your tale of woe or some other erroneous perception is standing in the way. So to make changes you first have to be willing and able to see these underlying patterns, recognize them for what they are, and then get rid of them.

PASSION

Often we are told, "Follow your passion and the rest will follow." But this is not necessarily true. There are plenty of "starving artists" out there who can relate to this. And there are plenty of people who follow their passion right into bankruptcy. In the transitional time we find ourselves living in now, we are being challenged not only to follow our passion, but to *connect* it with something. We are being challenged to come into alignment.

Passion cannot exist long by itself. To manifest into form it needs a partner. You cannot create a child only with the power of your mind, your creativity, and your positive thinking. To effectively manifest here, we need to learn to co-create.

What or whom do you choose as your co-creating partner?

WHAT DO YOU MEAN CO-CREATE?

The term "co-create" has been become a popular buzz word but it is a term that is widely misunderstood. To co-create you must be willing to come into alignment and combine your own unique ingredients with:

(1) Your life's purpose;
(2) Your higher self or higher wisdom and;
(3) Universal will.

CONNECT THE DOTS

To have your life come together into your own bigger picture, you must connect the dots. Every child looking at a "connect the dot" picture knows this. If you don't draw the actual lines between 1 and 2 and 3 and so forth, you're just staring at a bunch of dots on a page. They appear to be random dots on a page that have no real form. It's when you start connecting them together that you end up with and discover the real picture, the real form. That is the both the challenge and the joy.

While you are residing in this physical form, the keys to connecting those "dots" are in your chakras. You are being challenged to connect those energies, and starting from the root, let go of anything that blocks the pathway of that connection, and then multi-dimensionally integrate your mind, body, and spirit. It's not hard. It's a process. The other choice is to keep staring at dots on a page wondering where the flesh of your life is.

CREATING FROM YOUR ROOT

On this planet we cannot yet visualize a flowering plant in our minds and have it poof out into existence. You must begin with dot #1. You must start at the root. If you don't do that—start at the beginning—you can end up with a scribbled, chaotic mess. Instead, go in order and end up with a cohesive result.

Energy here is designed to begin its journey as a seed, an embryo. Then it gets planted—or "implanted"—and gets fed and nourished from the root system. The energy flows up the formed stem of a plant, leaves eventually sprout, then buds, and THEN at the right time the flower develops, and from that ultimately the fruit. To accomplish this and partake of the juicy harvest, you must begin creating from the root, the core, the base of who you are.

I DON'T KNOW WHO I AM

Sure you do. Who you are is not necessarily what you do and quite probably isn't if you're reading this book. The answer to who you are is found at your emotional core. If you feel as if you don't know who you are, you are in some way disconnected from your emotional body.

Are you avoiding your emotional core? We learn or are taught to detach from our emotions as some kind of protection, as a way to fit in better with the tribe and do what they're doing. But we need our emotional body in order to effectively manifest. And there are a lot of light workers and people in general who clearly aren't doing what their tribe is doing and therefore feel emotional disconnection in that way and on that tribal level as well.

To reconnect with who you are, go back to childhood and start putting the pieces together. Connect the dots. Were you perhaps told something like, "Children are seen and not heard?" Were you told to "Stop crying!" Did you suffer mental, physical, or verbal abuse? These are all things that would take you farther and farther away from the very essence of who you are.

Sometimes it can be painful to reconnect to our emotional selves long buried. That's why some people avoid doing so. But doing so is necessary to the healing process, to rediscovering who you are, *and* to the process of manifesting.

Within the structure of the emotional body, everything is built in layers. So engaging in this reconnection process will simply take you through the layers. The physical body is designed this way for a good reason.

Rediscovering yourself and any long stuffed down emotions will not be like ripping off a sticky, painful bandage. The process can be a gentle movement through each layer. If you don't feel as if you know who you are, this work is worth doing and needs to be done in order to get to the root.

WHAT WEALTHY PEOPLE KNOW

What do wealthy people know that you don't know? What do they have that you don't? More money?

One thing they have, besides perhaps more money, is the very important knowledge that they are already wealthy. They may not know who they are *without* their money, but that's not really the issue.

Because they already know without question that they are wealthy, they have—with or without being consciously aware of it—freed themselves (or been freed) to create more money.

Having money allows us to move from "survival mode" into "creative mode." When we are not in survival mode, the energy of money is then free to travel up the pipeline and become form made manifest.

For you to effectively manifest, you need to open a pipeline to the energy of money. You need to move yourself out of the thought pattern of survival mode. And it is a thought pattern. No matter what situation you find yourself in, survival mode is a perception, even if it doesn't feel that way.

If you see it that way, it's easier to move out of that perception rather than staying stuck in the emotion of the fear that survival mode can create within your root. And that is the fear that has the power to immobilize you if you allow it to do so.

If you could then, as a first step, move your linear mind into knowing that you are already wealthy, you could begin to free yourself as well.

THE ENERGY OF CREATION

Money attracts more money. Right? That's true. But that's not exactly the whole equation. When you free up the energy housed in the 2nd chakra—your creative ideas—*and* you free up the energy that lives in the root, you can combine these and then "birth" them more easily.

Where people get stuck in the birthing process of bringing their creative ideas to fruition, AND "making" more money in the process, is in not understanding that the energy of CREATION lives in the root, unlike what you've been taught. . . that it lives in some obscure place behind you and/or in your spine. Think about it. To make a child, to create life, you need to engage your root, not the base of your spine.

But survival, the primal instinct to live, and the innate instinct of fear—fight or flight—also reside in the root.

So it's when these energies—the energy of creation, the energy of survival, and the creative life force energy that lives in the 2nd chakra—oppose one another, this is when you have money troubles.

MONEY: A PRIMARY RELATIONSHIP

Your relationship with money is like any other relationship. Examine it. What's the balance of power? What do your current and past romantic relationships look like? Are they reckless, passionate, and out of control? Are they stingy and emotionally bereft or withholding? Do they bear interest? Does money control you? Does it have power over you? Do you control it? Are you a helpless victim? Are you a manipulator?

Any successful relationship requires energies

that work together in harmony. It is essential if you want to financial freedom, that you bring your relationship with money into focus and balance, and change those things that do not work.

In order to effectively do this, you absolutely must get to the root of the matter. That doesn't mean that you need to go into therapy for years and years. And you don't have to hash and rehash. It means that you need to look at a very base level where you're stuck and why you're stuck there. Who taught you what you know about money? And more importantly, who taught you what you know about RELATIONSHIPS? And what exactly is your primal, primary fear regarding both money AND relationships?

The past has shaped your present. It doesn't need to have any influence on the future. But like clothing you've stuffed in a drawer and forgotten about, the clothing is still in there whether you even remember you have it, or whether you bring it out and wear it or not.

At some point you have to address that which is taking up space in your bureau, because if you want to make room for anything else to come in, you'll be faced with doing so. There is no avoiding it. Your other choice is to buy a completely new dresser or bureau. It's a choice.

You are already wealthy. Know it with your linear mind first. Accept it into your energy field; into your emotional body. Embrace it with your heart and soul. And then live it.

NICHOLAS

Nicholas had some vague suspicions about his current accountant, Frank, but he had no real proof of anything. It was just a feeling. If the guy was stealing from him, he sure was good at it. Very slick. *But, really, did the man think he was stupid?* He really hated it when that happened.

When he and Lucky had been together. . .well, she had done a lot of things for him, taken care of a lot of things for him, taken care of *him.* He, in turn, was now slowly beginning to realize he had taken her for granted. He didn't deserve her. *Damn it*, maybe he really *was* stupid.

ANTHONY

Anthony slunk back into the grey shadows, his handsome, yet scarred face gathered into a sinister growl. He was a master of disguise and a master at hiding in obscurity. He had followed Barbie and Frankie to their love nest high in the hills. In fact, he'd been following Barbie or had her followed for years. She just didn't know it.

And the other thing she didn't know was that he had stashed their child in Sicily where she was safe with trusted relatives and Barbie would never, ever find her there. Never.

There, in the shadows of Frank's rented house, Anthony had lurked and watched and listened for as long as he could until he just wanted to throw up. Anthony was well aware of Barbie's escapades over the years. But this one was just over the top. *His own cousin, for Crissake! Had the woman no shame? She was still his wife. Didn't she know that?*

Even though Frank was a second cousin and a few times removed even, he was still a cousin. The fact that Barbie had no way of knowing this didn't matter to Anthony. His hot Sicilian blood boiled like thick, overcooked tomato sauce ready to spill over onto the stove.

He should go in there, grab her by the hair, beat her to a pulp and throw her half dead, half naked carcass on the side of the road like the wild animal that she was.

Anthony somehow managed to get control of his rising rage because he had to for right now.

But Barbie would definitely get what she deserved. And maybe that cousin of his too.

ELAYNE

Over the past few years, Elayne had done an excellent job of conquering her fears and everything else. Through the practice of yoga her Kundalini had risen gently, just like the big, beautiful muffins made and sold at her now very successful yoga studio. She was happy.

In addition, she had a magazine, a good husband, and lots of money. With the money she had earned, she had even put herself through medical school. She was now in the first year of her residency. And after producing and starring in several yoga videos, she had recently been asked to star in her own television program. It was all like a dream come true. She was successful beyond her wildest dreams. And she deserved it.

Her fast paced, full-bodied life could seem overwhelming to some, but through years of daily and steadfast discipline she had learned to not let anything overwhelm her or scare her. She had learned to take things one at a time and in stride. She felt she possessed a certain degree of enlightenment. And because of that she never bit off more than she could chew.

DESERVING

There is a lot of damage that can be done in the root chakra and a great deal of that damage, and subsequent distortion, starts in childhood. If, for example, you had parents who said things to you like, "You deserve a spanking," and then followed suit with that action, you can probably relate to this. You begin to believe that you deserve to be abused. As we grow into adulthood, no one tells us to get rid of this. So we hang onto it and absorb it in as truth into the deep layers of our emotional body.

We then may have a series of experiences and relationships that reinforce this feeling of being deserving of some kind of abuse. And we may come to crave it or we may come to twist it up into some distorted sense of love: "Love is abusive." We will then and therefore attract it.

So our basic root chakra feelings can get damaged and skewed, and distorted, and can become so early on.

The truth is that love is indeed *not* abusive. And the truth is that no one is deserving of any kind of abuse. But we may attract it to us, and continue to attract it to us, due to stuck energy patterns in our root. We will attract that which is familiar. Attraction is a frequency and a vibration.

As well, remember, that the energy of money resides in the root, so we may come to also attract a job or career in which we feel abused in some way, as this pattern of abuse is simply familiar to us. It's why we stay in jobs or relationships that are not healthy or productive. *At least we know this pattern.* But this is exactly what is in the way of our success.

LUCKY AND BARBARA

Lucky and Barbara had gotten into a deep discussion one night. Lucky was exasperated. It had been almost five months and Barbara still wasn't working. Lucky had been paying for everything, food, utilities, everything. *Where had she not been clear?* she wondered. *Good grief*, she had even paid to have Barbie's Mercedes fixed. And she often found herself cleaning up after Barbie's little dog, Toto, as well.

Plus, the casita was always in disarray. Lucky refused to clean it up, but it perturbed her greatly. After all, *what else did the woman have to do all day?* She could at least keep the casita in order. It seemed like a reflection of Barbie's life: A total mess. *Did Barbara really expect her to be able to keep on carrying her like a pack mule? And for how long?* Barbie was a grown woman and she needed to work, just like everyone else. There wasn't any reason for her not to work doing something, anything. Waitressing, scrubbing toilets, warehouse work even. If she had a bad back, it would only have been from too much rolling around in the hay.

Lucky noted that Barbie had been spending plenty of time with Frank, literally screwing around. And Barbie looked marvelous, tan and healthy and glowing, almost like the perpetual bling she sported. If she ditched the tight clothes, she shouldn't have too much trouble getting hired somewhere. *Snap out of it!*

* * * * *

So what if she spent time enjoying herself? Was she supposed to be miserable? Barbie thought. Lucky just didn't understand. She deserved a break after all she'd been through. And she just couldn't seem to find any psychic work even though she had tried numerous times. She just didn't have any other marketable skills that she could think of and she certainly wasn't going to go wash dishes somewhere.

Lucky suggested that she go back to Carla's store and ask again.

"That Carla just doesn't like me," Barbie pouted. "People, you know. They just don't want the truth."

"Oh, I'm sure that's not it, Babs. Carla is a sweetheart. Can you please, please try again?" Lucky pleaded.

Lucky had spent the past five months working very diligently, finishing up and polishing her new screenplay. It was finally ready. And it was excellent if she did say so herself. She had a good feeling about this one. A really good feeling. Her agent agreed.

Barbie whined, "Sis, didn't you say your astrology chart was all full of squares and oppositions? Well, since we're twins, we must have the same chart, right? With all that's going on, I just can't seem to get off of square one. Nothing's happening, no matter what I do. "I'll have to wait until things clear up and Saturn gets off my back. December, maybe. The energy should be better by then."

Lucky rolled her eyes and it was all she could do to keep from screaming at her twin. She was furious and didn't feel like being anyone's mother.

"No more excuses, Barbara." We can't wait until December. You need to try to find something *now*," Lucky said firmly, using her sister's formal name.

"But I'm *trying*," Barbie whined.

"No you're *not*," Lucky returned emphatically. "Just please go check again with Carla."

The two glared at each other for a few moments in silence. There was no way for Barbara to win and she knew it. She nodded. "Okay. Will do, Lucky," Barbara replied, her head low. "Will do."

The tension thick as fog, Barbara quickly changed the subject. They started talking about Barbie's favorite subject: Men. But Barbie poured her heart out to her sister then, not realizing how much she had wanted to do this, but had never found quite the right time. Lucky had been so focused on her work as of late. Now was as good as a time as any. She definitely didn't want to talk about getting a job anymore.

Barbara opened up and spilled her guts. She'd been too ashamed, too bottled up to have shared any of this with Lucky before. She couldn't handle anyone's judgments. But something just felt right to tell her now.

Barbara told Lucky all about Anthony and her missing daughter and all she had been through over the past several years. She finished with, "And I don't even know if I'm still married, really."

Lucky stared at her in astonishment, blue eyes wide, and mouth agape. *What a bizarre story. She'd had no idea. None.* No wonder Babs did the things she did. *Still. . .*

"Why don't you go see an attorney and find out what your options are, Babs? You know, Carla's husband can probably help you with this. At least he can probably point you in the right direction. Maybe you get Anthony declared dead, maybe you need to get a formal divorce. Maybe Carlos knows a good private investigator. I don't know. You should talk to him. And usually these initial consultations are free. You should at least talk to him and see what he has to say."

Barbie's eyes lit up with a small ray of gleaming, blue hope. She nodded in agreement. Yes, it made sense. She would do it.

"And," Lucky said with a slight edge of sarcasm that she just couldn't resist, "I think Carlos' office is actually in the same building as Frank's." "Next time you're up that way, see if he can fit you in."

HEALTHY BOUNDARIES

In order to not engage in the co-dependent relationship of enabling, we need to learn to have and make healthy boundaries. Even when we are clear in our boundaries, there are still those who will purposefully step over them, try to break them down, and act as if they are not there. This is where you have to learn to detach.

It is important to understand this kind of detachment. This is not about detaching from your own emotional body *or* from the person (if the person not honoring your boundaries is someone you care about). It's not about closing your emotional doors and windows. It's not about that. You are detaching from the *pattern*, not the person or how you feel about them. Ask yourself if you are the doorway or the doormat?

It is essential that you learn to make healthy boundaries. *Essential.* But it's one of the hardest things to do because the truth is that no one likes anyone with boundaries. And in our root also lives our longing for acceptance.

Those that don't respect other people's boundaries usually have no boundaries themselves, consistently put themselves into the role of victim, and wonder what the trouble is. The following simple verbiage should help, because it assists you in beginning the process of making healthy boundaries in a non-confrontational manner.

"I am willing," or "I am not willing." Use these phrases whenever you feel your boundaries are not being honored. Get them into your vocabulary as a matter of course.

Keep in mind that what our goal is with making boundaries is "boundaries, not barriers." We don't want to stick ourselves in a place where we are unforgiving and rigid. That isn't it. It's more about the necessity to make *and keep* a healthy boundary when the buttons of our patterns are being pushed. Got it?

PATTERNS

You could come to a complete understanding of events in your life if you could understand and are willing to look at your patterns, along with what pushes the buttons or triggers those patterns. The natural tendency is to do what we are comfortable doing. And that comfort zone is built upon our root chakra patterns.

For example, we can move ourselves geographically yet find that the same patterns and circumstances keep showing up. When we move, we think we are in for a new beginning.

However, anything that you haven't *solved at the root* is going to be right in your face no matter where you are. And therefore you will create the same scenario in the new space, no matter what you do. So now is the time to examine the root and the patterns that live there. Unless you do, you will automatically manifest and try to create from your patterns, however dysfunctional.

DYSFUNCTIONAL PATTERNS IN FAMILIES

Our patterns are created in childhood. We take our cues and follow along with those in our tribe because we want and need to fit in. This we do for survival. But the patterns of your family or tribe do not have to be your patterns. You can choose to not engage in those patterns if you don't like them.

Remember as well, that your family is in essence your "soul group." Groups of souls agree to incarnate at the same time to work on certain patterns and lessons. To master these has the effect of moving the entire soul group to a higher place, spiritually speaking. There is opportunity to transform, not just individually, but as an entire group.

What may be important for some "light workers" to understand is that some souls agreed to come in here simply to be present at this particular time, to help *humanity* as a group, rather than a particular family. So in these instances, for example, one may feel like they do not know their family, like they are doing something completely different, like they don't fit in with what the family is doing.

This can be unnerving and un-grounding, because the root will tell us that we should fit in with these people. And we don't know why we don't. Consequently, many years can be spent on this effort of trying to fit in or understand why so and so acts the way they do or did the things they did to you.

But the truth is that in these cases, you aren't supposed to fit in. The patterns of these people perhaps are just foreign to you—to your soul—and no matter how you try, you're just not going to be able to adopt these patterns. Why would you want to?

Now that you know what this is about, detach and get on with your real purpose in life, which is much bigger than trying to fit the square peg into the round hole.

CARLOS

Carlos pulled into the small parking lot in front of his office and turned off the black Lexus. The big law firm he was with maintained huge formal offices in a shiny, reflective skyscraper downtown. But this was a satellite office the firm had recently opened; an older home converted into office space that was not far from his own home. The location was far more convenient and Carlos was almost, but not quite, totally moved in.

If he had to guess, he would say the house was maybe a Modern Victorian or maybe it was a Craftsman style, something on this order. Carlos, not being that well versed on architectural styles wasn't quite sure. And he didn't care. All he cared about was that the space was roomy, pleasant, and conducive to getting work done, which it definitely was.

The big house sported a wide front porch extending all the way across the breadth of the dwelling, and the exterior paint was done in several bright, beachy type colors. That suited him fine as well. They were happy colors. And Carlos was unquestionably happy.

Carlos needed to pick up some papers he had forgotten to bring home with him and he needed them now. While he was there, he thought, he'd also finish up a few other quick things before he went home.

It was late, it was dark, but he noticed the other black Lexus was there as well. He knew it belonged to Frank, the accountant who was one of the other tenants in the building. Upon one of their first meetings not long ago, they even had joked about it. *Twin cars.*

As polite and as friendly as Carlos tried to be—even poking his head into Frank's office from time to time to say hello—there was just something about this Frank that he didn't quite trust. He wasn't sure what it was exactly, as he couldn't quite put his finger on it, but there was something. . .shady about the man.

And he certainly didn't look like any accountant Carlos had ever met. In fact, from a distance he thought, he and Frank looked somewhat alike. They had similar dark, crisp hair, dark eyes, and general build. *Extraño,* Carlos had thought. *Bizarre.* Well, whatever. At least no one would ever mistake him, Carlos, for an accountant. That much he knew.

The converted house was set back a little from the road, the driveway semi-circular, and the small but adequate parking lot set off to one side was bordered all the way back and around by a forest of thick trees and heavy foliage.

Carlos got out of the Lexus, made his way across the parking lot and up the few steps that were in front of the building. Upon entering he could hear muffled noises and voices coming from Frank's office. He pointedly ignored them and made his way into his own office. He knew who was in there and it was none of his business, even if he did understand on some level. *People were just quirky.* But it was his opinion that they should do whatever they were doing elsewhere.

Barbara, Lucky's twin sister had come to see Carlos just the week before. Carlos had almost fallen off his chair when he first met her. She looked so much like Lucky, and yet at the same time, so much about her was definitely not like Lucky. This one had some hard edges to her that Lucky just didn't have.

Since that meeting, he recognized her as the girl he'd seen coming in and out of Frank's office a few times before. He was actually relieved to find out it hadn't been Lucky, which is what he'd thought at first. He knew she and Nicholas had been broken up several months ago, but the thought of Lucky with Frank, well, it just nauseated him for some reason. *She was too good for him.* This Barbara, now, that was another matter. Barbara and Frank just seemed like they fit together like long lost puzzle pieces under someone's desk. Or bed.

After listening to Barbie's story last week, Carlos was able to give her some good, solid advice and said he would refer her to those that could help. Carlos was very connected in his own way. And her story, he thought, was something else. Undoubtedly bizarre. She had also, for some reason he couldn't begin to fathom, related the story of her near death experience and how she had become psychic shortly thereafter. Not sure what that had to do with anything, he said he would try to help.

BARBIE AND FRANKIE

Barbie sat on Frankie's lap facing him, and kissed him full on the mouth trying to distract him and talk him into staying at the office. Even though it was ostensibly more private, she didn't like that creepy old rented house he lived in, not one bit. She always felt as if someone was watching them there. As many times as she'd been to that house now, she always had that same feeling. The office was definitely more exciting anyway.

Frank pushed her gently away. "Come on, woman. I have work I have to get done tonight." He hadn't been expecting her and they'd "done it" once already.

"You know I walked here, Frankie, from the

yoga studio. It's too dark for me to walk home alone now."

She pulled him into another kiss, this one more passionate than the one before, and he relented, allowing himself to fall momentarily under her spell. He was unable to resist her particular charms and really didn't want to.

Besides, she was ecstatic, happy as could be and a little celebration was certainly in order. She had finally found work that very day. Lucky would be ecstatic too.

But it wasn't psychic work. She had actually gone to Carla's again, as promised, albeit several days after she and Lucky had had that very tense discussion. But Carla still wasn't hiring.

While there, she had decided to explore the other quaint shops in the area and she had wandered into a nearby yoga studio. The sign in the window had said "Help Wanted: Baker." *She could do that!*

Elayne, also at first mistaking her for Lucky, had hired her on the spot after Barbie had shared her quite special muffin recipe, and she was to start baking muffins on Monday. Soon, she'd be "in the dough" so to speak.

Frankie suddenly pushed her away again.

"Wait. . . stop. . . .Barbie. Stop. I have something for you."

Her voice husky with desire, she murmured, "Yes, I *know*, darling."

"No! Not that. . .yet. . .wait!" He was serious. She stopped.

He leaned over with one long arm and reached into the bottom desk drawer. He'd been waiting for the right moment to do this and now was as good as any. He had something special for her. *Only for her*. He'd never given any other woman such a thing. They hadn't been worth the risk.

From the drawer, Frank pulled out a long, red velvet jewelry box and handed it to her.

"Open it."

Barbie's china blue eyes widened in shock as she opened the spring hinged box and stared in stunned disbelief at the gleaming treasure that lay inside.

Nestled inside, on a bed of white satin, was an exquisite, blood red ruby necklace, accented expertly with sparkling diamonds. She'd never seen anything so beautiful in her entire life. There must have been fifteen whole carats of gemstone on this piece, maybe more.

"These are *real*!" she exclaimed. Every woman always knows what's real and what's not. "It's breathtaking, Frankie!" she said excitedly, her big eyes growing even wider. He must think the world of her to give her something like this. No one ever had before. She'd always had to settle for costume bling and maybe that's why she wore so much of it. It's what she was used to. But this. . .*this* was *amazing. It must be worth a fortune.*

He smiled. "Yes, I know. Amazing. . .*like you, Barbie.* And one condition. I only want you to wear this for *me*. Only for me."

The necklace had been stolen years ago and in a different country. So he was reasonably sure the heat was off by now, but still, ever cautious, he wasn't willing to take any chances. Still stunned, Barbie nodded in silent agreement.

"Now. . ." he said authoritatively. "Take off the rest of your clothes. All of them. Put the ice on. And. . . let's start cooking."

Barbie heart melted. She obliged. And then some.

CARLA

Carla knew something was wrong even before she heard the sirens. She and her Carlos were so connected, how could it be otherwise? She just couldn't imagine what that "something wrong" could be.

She stared in disbelief at the Death card which had slipped out from underneath her white satin pillow and onto the floor by the bed. She hadn't been doing a reading. She had actually been changing the sheets. She wanted a nice, fresh bed ready for when her Carlos returned from the office. And candlelight. She had lit some fragrant, red rose scented candles. She had plans. Big plans.

The telephone rang shrilly and further jangled Carla's already jumpy nerves. Their child was on an overnight sleepover. Carla hoped the "something wrong" didn't have anything to do with her boy. She answered the phone quickly, the red candles flickering with the movement of air.

It was Elayne. She was calling from the emergency room of the hospital where she was doing her residency.

Carla listened silently in stunned disbelief to what Elayne had to say, not quite fully comprehending or integrating it all. And then without one word dropped the phone onto the floor. It fell from her shaking hand and landed right on top of that dreadful card of *La Muerte* which she hadn't yet picked up. There it lay, motionless on the ground.

Carla herself felt frozen in time; inert, immobilized, and out of control. But somehow she knew this wasn't just regular old death. She knew in her heart this was murder. *Asesinato. Who would want to kill her dear, sweet, Carlos, the father of her child, the love of her life? The world had gone mad. Loco!*

CARLOS

Carlos had finished up as best as he could at the office for the evening. Not that the walls were so very thin, but the couple in Frank's office were just so very loud. *Dios! Offices were for working.* He hoped this wasn't going to become an ongoing habit for them.

Carlos gathered up the last of his papers and put them in his briefcase. These two were very distracting and he wanted very much to get home to his Carla.

Finally, it seemed, they had taken a break—at

least for now—the ensuing silence almost surreal.

He grabbed his briefcase with one hand, turned off the lights with the other, and after locking the door to his office behind him, Carlos went down the wide hallway and out to the parking lot, locking the front office door behind him as well.

It was a very dark, moonless night and the old, leafy trees from the abutting forest cast even more shadows on the jet black asphalt. He noted that the twin Lexus was no longer there. *They must have finally left*, he thought. *That explained the eerie silence.*

As he approached his own Lexus he pressed the keyless remote, and the flash of the lights—or maybe it was the flash from the gun that shot him—was one of the last things he remembered. In the still surreal silence, he hadn't *heard* anything at all.

One of the bullets had hit him in the neck; at least that's how it seemed to him. Now Carlos was lying face down in the black driveway of his office in an ever increasing, dark pool of his own blood. Lots of blood seemed to be pouring out of him; his whole life rapidly seeping away. He hadn't seen his life flash before his eyes like people say happens. Maybe that was a good thing.

Strangely, the last thing he remembered thinking before he passed out was, *God, if he was going to have a near death experience, he hoped he wouldn't wake up to be psychic.*

ELAYNE

Even with all of the other things happening in her life, Elayne was in her medical school residency. She actually wasn't sure if she was going to make it through or not, but she was going to try. She was currently doing a rotation in the emergency room. Until they brought in the gunshot victim, the night had been relatively quiet with only a few routine cases.

Elayne froze for a moment, temporarily immobilized, and stared in gaping horror at the bloody man on the gurney. It was someone she knew. Carlos. *Omygod.*

ANTHONY

Anthony crouched low in the dense woodland that abutted the office property where he'd been for about ten minutes. He shifted his weight to try to get a better vantage point. He had been waiting for the right circumstances, plotting, and now was the perfect time. He was going to kill Frankie. Cousin or no, Frank was not going to get away with sleeping with his wife any longer. *No*.

Anthony's rage had been seething on the stove of anger and jealousy for weeks. His red, hot fury seemed to have reached the point of simply uncontrollable. Boiling over it was.

He knew Barbie and Frankie had been trysting at Frank's office just lately, instead of at the rented house in the hills, but it was usually during the day. Now they were here at night, and the dark, moonless evening, and the helpful cover of thick trees made it the perfect night for a murder.

FRANKIE AND BARBIE

Their raw appetites sated at least for the moment, Frankie and Barbie got dressed, left the office and got a quick bite to eat. *Barbie was voraciously hungry all the time,* he thought. Afterward, Frank drove Barbie home and then headed back to the office to finish his work, thinking amusedly the whole way there about her many, many appetites.

* * * * *

ANTHONY

Anthony saw Frankie come out of the office and walk over to his black Lexus. A hot, crimson rage seemed to bubble up from somewhere deep inside him and rose up all the way to the top of his head, blinding him to all reason. And beyond that he just saw more red. He fired three shots at Frankie in rapid succession and saw him go down. He had expertly hit the mark. *Success!* Anthony smiled sardonically to himself in supreme satisfaction and ran for the hills.

FRANKIE

Frank pulled into the driveway of the office and knew immediately that something wasn't right. Carlo's car was still here and it was quite late now. *He should have been gone by now*, Frank thought to himself. *What is that on the ground?*

In stunned disbelief, Frank parked, exited his Lexus and there saw Carlos lying on the ground in a pool of oozing blood. The body was still warm and Carlos, unbelievably, still had a weak pulse. *This must have just happened.*

Frankie reached inside his pocket, pulled out his cell phone and called 911. As he waited for the ambulance, Frankie shuddered in the waning warmth of the evening. "I think this was meant for me," he said aloud to no one.

CARLA

The things that were going around in Carla's head as she raced to the hospital weren't anything she wanted to ever share with anyone. She couldn't believe she was even thinking these things as her love was very possibly dying. *What was wrong with her?* She felt like she was in a "bizarre table." *Tableau,* that was, she corrected herself. She really was trying to be better with her English.

All she could think of was *now what?* Her mind was racing and spinning around in an endless circle. What if her beloved Carlos actually died? She couldn't conceive of it. Her store was popular and successful, but not successful enough to maintain their oceanfront lifestyle.

That she was aware of. And there was no contingency plan in place. She was even more aware of that fact. Carla wasn't sure what that contingency plan might even be. Life insurance maybe? As ridiculous as it may have seemed, they hadn't thought that far ahead. They had talked about it, but hadn't ever done anything about it.

Who wants to think about the unthinkable, especially when they were still young? They were just living their lives, like everyone else.

Carla felt more powerless at the moment than she'd ever felt in her entire life. Carlos just had to be okay. He just had to be. *He would be. She had to snap out of it and bring herself back together.* And to her own surprise, she did.

* * * * *

WHAT IS POWER?

Some people would say that money is power. After all, money as power is a pretty powerful perception here, and a perception we have firmly believed in for a very long time. But you can have no money whatsoever and still have power. People can steal your money but they cannot steal your light unless you allow them to do so.

Some people would say that knowledge is power. But you can have no formal education whatsoever and still have power. There is great power in what you *think.*

Some people would say that beauty is power. But you can still have power even if you are the most physically revolting, ugly person on the planet. Our perceptions of what real beauty is remain skewed and we persist in Photoshopping our illusions and distortions of perfection, sometimes to the extreme.

Some people would say that love is power. And of course it is. But our perceptions of love often include conditions, manipulation, and abuse.

The truth is that power—in earthly terms—is essentially an illusion. The real power is the power of who you are in your spirit. That is because this is something that no one can take from you—ever—unless you allow them to do so.

At the place we find ourselves now, it is the things that we *believe* have power over us that have power. And like Dorothy in *The Wizard of Oz*, you can call that power back to you any time you'd like and no matter where you are.

You just have to be keenly aware of it, figure out where you've given it away, and then know what to do about it, i.e., how to call it back to you and how to use it to get to where you want to go.

In life, money can come and go. Who are you without it? There is power in knowing that. In life, there are varying degrees and pieces of paper that tell us who we are. Who are you without those papers? There is power in the knowledge of this.

In life, physical beauty can come and go and can fade with time. Who are you with or without wrinkles? Who are you with or without physical weight? There is power in knowing this and seeing beyond what we think we see.

In life, love in various forms comes and goes. What does unconditional love look like for you? There is power in that.

So what is power? Your spirit already knows, has always known, and will always know.

EPILOGUE

While happily baking muffins for Elayne's yoga studio, Barbara wrote a cookbook, "Barbie's Batters," which got published by a large, well known publisher. It sold over 1 million copies. She got a hefty advance for her next cookbook and even had a regular cooking segment on Elayne's TV program for which she was paid very handsomely and made a lot of dough.

Anthony was located, arrested, indicted, convicted, and sentenced to life in prison for the attempted murder of Carlos Ortega. The child, Francesca, whom Anthony had taken to Sicily and renamed, Enna, was found and returned to the custody of Barbara, her biological mother.

Kenetha got used to being called "Kenneth" by Carla, and got a permanent position at Carla's Tarot Dream. When the shooting happened, she did the astrology of the day as well as an astrological profile on both Anthony and Carlos. As it turned out. . . "the chart says."

Carlos fully recovered after several months. It was a miracle from above. And Carlos and Carla didn't lose anything. Their house didn't even burn down from the lit candles Carla forgot to blow out. They gained a whole new appreciation and outlook on life and engaged in some good, solid financial planning.

Lucky's screenplay hit it big. Really, *really* big. She recommended Frank to write the music for the movie score and this finally got him on the musical map.

Frankie retired his thieving ways, and after her divorce from Anthony, he married Barbie in a destination wedding on his private island. But he did keep the stolen jewels. All of them. There are some things that just do not change.

Lucky and Nicholas got back together. And they stayed together. Nicholas? He's *still* a work in progress.

And our root chakras? Still there.

Date Muffins

1/2 cup bran
1/4 cup wheat germ
2 cups flour
3/4 cup sugar
1/2 teaspoon salt
1/2 teaspoon baking soda
2 eggs
1 cup milk (do not use skim milk)
1 teaspoon lemon juice
1 T sour cream
2 T honey
Splash of vanilla
1/3 cup vegetable oil
1 cup dates, pitted and chopped
1/2 cup walnuts (may omit)

Preheat oven to 350 degrees. Combine dry ingredients in large mixing bowl. By hand, beat in eggs, milk, lemon juice, sour cream. Stir in honey, vanilla and oil. Stir in dates and nuts. Fill muffin cups. Bake 20 minutes or until golden brown. **Blueberry muffins**: Substitute fresh blueberries for dates. Ditto for **Cherry muffins.**

Date Muffin recipe © Dyan Garris – *Voice of the Angels Cookook: Talk to Your Food! Intuitive Cooking*

OTHER BOOKS BY DYAN GARRIS

MONEY AND MANIFESTING

Best-Selling and Award Winning Finalist

Four days after reading Money & Manifesting, we manifested money. . .and it just keeps rolling in! ~ Laurie B.

MUSIC AND GUIDED MEDITATION CDS BY DYAN GARRIS

Soul soothing CD series of music and guided meditation for vibrational attunement of mind, body, and spirit.

Dyan Garris products available at CDBaby.com, Amazon.com, DyanGarris.com, or your local CD retailer.

A Healing Journey – The Voice of the Angels
Moment by Moment – Music for the Soul
Reflection
Patterns
Illusions
Connections
* * * * *
Release CD
Eight: Music for Ascension
Spiritus Sanctus Vol. 1 & 2
Perfect Pathways, Vol. 1 & 2

RELAXATION DVD
DOORS TO THE SOUL
BY DYAN GARRIS

Automatically balance your energy field in ten minutes with this unique relaxation DVD by Dyan Garris

I just got done watching your DVD. It's amazing! I am totally and fully energized and yet more relaxed than ever. I can get done what I need to get done now. Thank you for this! ~ Julie Z.

ABOUT THE AUTHOR: Dyan Garris is a visionary mystic, voice recognition psychic, and trance channel medium who reads directly from the Akashic Records. Her specialties are chakra balance, manifesting, and teaching people what is missing from the way manifesting was taught. She has created a Spiritual Toolbox of products that work together for multi-dimensional and integrative living. This includes a multiple award nominated CD series of New Age music and guided meditation with several #1 charting songs, and a double accredited chakra balance certification course which is also 50 hours of continuing education through NCBTMB. She is also the author and artist of "Voice of the Angels – A Healing Journey Spiritual Cards" and several other books, including the award winning finalist and best- selling book *Money and Manifesting*. **Free angel card readings online** in English and Spanish, and a phone psychic network with real psychics available at: www.VoiceOfTheAngels.com

www.DyanGarris.com

www.ingramcontent.com/pod-product-compliance
Lightning Source LLC
LaVergne TN
LVHW051121080426
835510LV00018B/2159

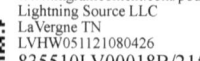